JACKSON'S WEST

Miles
50 100 200

PICTURE MAKER

OF THE

OLD WEST

BY

CLARENCE S. JACKSON

CHARLES SCRIBNER'S SONS, NEW YORK
CHARLES SCRIBNER'S SONS, LTD., LONDON
1947

THE life of my father, William Henry Jackson, spanned practically a century. He was ninety-nine years of age when he passed from us. The years of his life paralleled the development of photography, and practically the whole of his life was spent in applying the camera to what he saw.

Dean of American photographers at the time of his death, honored by scientific and professional societies here and abroad, he always looked upon his work in the mountain regions of the West as his great contribution to his art.

Always, as a recreation from the more prosaic settings or duties with which his later life required him to occupy himself, he would return to the West or to a portrayal of the West. In his studio, which he left one day in 1942 never to return, there stood on his easel an unfinished picture of a Western scene.

It was as a photographer that the public knew him. A whole generation viewed his camera studies through the stereoscope—and thus came to know and appreciate a West which most of them never visited. Enlarged copies of his pictures of the West hung in business offices throughout America, and in hotels in Bombay, and Calcutta. His photographs of the wonders of the Yellowstone region, the first ever taken, were the clinching argument in the move to have Congress create the Yellowstone National Park.

What is not so well known is the fact that, even when he had no camera, he none the less portrayed the life of the West as he saw it. As he cracked the whip over a bull train lumbering along the Oregon Trail, or as he plunged after stampeding horses on the Old Spanish Trail, his eyes saw pictures, and before the light of day had faded he had transferred them to a notebook or any piece of paper that happened to be handy. Those pencil sketches, carefully preserved along with his diary, are also a part of his picture record of the West. I have, I think properly, had them reproduced in this volume. And as life gave him leisure, my father added still another form of interpretation to his hurried sketches and his carefully posed photographs. In water-color paintings based on his sketches, his photographs, and his intimate knowledge of the country, he interpreted the early West with a spirit that few have equalled and none can question. In these pictures, the men, the horses and the pack mules of the trail days live again.

Such is the material that has gone into this volume. It is the vanished West as seen through the eyes, and as portrayed by the touch of a pencil, the placing of a camera, or the brush technique of a man who had known and loved the region.

In bringing together the representative pictures shown in this volume, I have, of course, leaned heavily upon the collections left to me by my father, but in addition I have been able to unearth a very large body of material in the Government archives, in public libraries and museums and in private hands—some of which I did not even know existed. From all these sources, and by the courtesy of Government officials and librarians and the many friends of my father, I have got together what I believe to be the best of his work for reproduction in this definitive showing of his picturing of the old West.

To my fellow photographers who look at these pictures but have had limited personal experience with pioneer photography, it may not be amiss to point out that practically all of them were made with the cumbersome and erratic equipment of seventy years ago. Heavy cameras, packs of plates and chemicals, dark tents and all the rest had often to be lugged up mountainsides where mules would not go—and they were lugged up on the back of the photographer.

The process of preparing a wet-plate and developing it called for great skill and art. I recall, as a small boy, seeing my father coat an 18 x 22 plate. He balanced it carefully on the thumb and fingers of his left hand, poured a pool of collodion in the far, left-hand corner of the plate, and then slowly worked the thick fluid about the edges and all over the plate until it reached the near, right-hand corner. So sure and careful was his hand that never a drop was spilled, nor was there any fluid left to be returned to the collodion bottle. This was hard enough to do in the studio, let alone on the top of a mountain in driving gales, after packing cameras, plates and plate-holders up over ledges slippery with ice and across treacherous fields of snow.

My only regret is that my father cannot see this selection from his life work. I do, however, take pleasure in passing the result of my own labors on to William Henry Jackson Griffith, great grandson of the artist, and to all others who may find this work of interest.

Although a page of formal acknowledgments gives credit to the institutions and the individuals who have so generously permitted me to use their material, I must add a personal word of gratitude to the following: Dr. Carl P. Russell, Chief Naturalist of the National Park Service; Dr. William E. Wrather and Mr. W. H. York of the United States Geological Survey; Dr. Neil Judd, Mr. J. E. Graf and Miss Tucker of the Smithsonian Institution; Mr. Horace M. Albright of New York City; Mr. G. G. Gilchrist of Denver, Colorado; Dr. Leroy Hafen and Mr. V. V. Peterson of the State Historical Society of Colorado; the Misses Wigginton and Aulls of the Denver Public Library; Messrs. H. R. Waddell and Fred Smith of the Edison Institute, Dearborn, Michigan; Messrs. Maxwell Perkins, R. V. Coleman and Joseph G. E. Hopkins of Charles Scribner's Sons.

C. S. JACKSON

Contents

ACKNOWLEDGMENT

The author is indebted to the following institutions and individuals for permission to reproduce photographs, paintings and sketches as specified.

Mr. Horace M. Albright, New York, N. Y., for the picture on page 153.

American Pioneer Trails Association, for the pictures on pages 1, 2, 3, 4, 5, 6 (*upper*), 7, 8, 9, 10, 22 (*upper*), 29 (*upper*).

Bureau of American Ethnology, Smithsonian Institution, Washington, D. C., for the pictures on pages 49, 50, 51, 52, 53, 57, 67, 68 (*upper*), 75, 78, 93, 94, 95, 195, 196 (*upper*), 197 (*lower*), 213 (*lower*), 227 (*upper*), 228, 288, 290.

Denver Public Library, Western Collection, Denver, Colorado, for the pictures on pages 55 (*lower*), 62 (*lower*), 111, 113 (*upper*), 178, 179 (*lower*), 199 (*upper*), 204, 215 (*lower*), 226, 235, 237 (*upper*), 241 (*lower*), 242, 243, 244, 245, 246, 247, 248, 249, 250, 251, 252, 253, 254, 255, 256 (*lower*), 257, 258, 259, 260, 263 (*lower*), 265 (*lower*), 266, 267, 268, 269, 270, 277, 292 (*lower*), 293, 294, 296, 299 (*lower*), 303.

Denver and Rio Grande Western Railroad Company, Denver, Colorado, for the pictures on pages 256 (*upper*), 263 (*upper*).

Eastman Kodak Company, Rochester, N. Y., for the pictures on pages 68 (*lower*), 96, 98 (*lower*), 99 (*upper left*), 102 (*lower*), 109 (*lower*), 125, 130, 132, 139, 141, 142, 166, 170 (*upper*), 175 (*upper*), 190, 191, 198 (*lower*), 202, 220 (*upper*), 223, 224 (*lower*), 232 (*upper*), 273, 274, 285 (*upper*), 286 (*upper*).

The Edison Institute, Dearborn, Michigan, for the pictures on pages 272, 275, 276, 278, 280, 298 (*upper*), 301.

Explorers' Club, New York, N. Y., for the picture on page 165.

Museum of Modern Art, New York, N. Y., for the pictures on pages 194 (*upper*), 229.

National Park Service, United States Department of the Interior, Chicago, Illinois, for the pictures on pages 6 (*lower*), 11, 12, 13, 14, 15, 16, 20 (*lower*), 21,

22 (*lower*), 23, 24 (*lower*), 25, 26, 27, 28, 30, 31, 32, 33 (*upper*), 34, 35, 36, 37, 38 (*upper*), 39, 40, 69 (*upper*), 83 (*upper*), 103 (*lower*), 116 (*upper*), 128 (*upper left*), 169 (*upper*), 186 (*lower*), 210, 222 (*upper*), 224 (*upper*), 230, 231, 237 (*lower*), 262, 281, 284 (*lower*), 295 (*lower*), 300.

Nebraska State Historical Society, Lincoln, Nebraska, for the picture on page 24 (*upper*).

State Historical Society of Colorado, Denver, Colorado, for the pictures on pages 295 (*upper*), 297 (*lower*).

Stereoscopic Collection, W. Whitehead Lytle, New York, N. Y., for the picture on page 232 (*lower*).

Union Pacific Historical Museum, Omaha, Nebraska, for the pictures on pages 43, 44, 45, 46, 47, 54 (*lower*), 60, 63 (*top*).

United States Geological Survey, United States Department of the Interior, Washington, D. C., for the pictures on pages 48, 54 (*upper*), 55 (*upper*), 56, 58, 59, 61, 62 (*upper*), 63 (*middle*), 63 (*bottom*), 64, 71, 84 (*lower*), 85, 86, 87, 88, 89, 90, 91, 97, 98 (*upper*), 99 (*upper right*), 99 (*lower*), 100, 102 (*upper*), 103 (*upper*), 104, 107, 110 (*upper*), 112, 113 (*lower*), 114, 115 (*lower*), 117, 118, 123, 124, 126, 128 (*upper right*), 128 (*lower*), 131, 133, 134, 135, 136, 137, 138, 140, 146, 147, 148, 149, 150, 151, 152, 154, 155, 156, 157, 158, 163, 164, 167, 168, 171, 174, 175 (*lower*), 176, 177, 179 (*upper*), 180, 181, 186 (*upper*), 198 (*upper*), 199 (*lower*), 200, 203, 205 (*upper*), 209, 215 (*upper*), 233 (*upper*), 241 (*upper*), 261, 282, 283, 284 (*upper*), 285 (*lower*), 286 (*lower*), 287, 292 (*upper*), 299 (*upper*).

PICTURE MAKER
OF THE
OLD WEST

CALL OF THE WEST

WHEN William Henry Jackson was a boy, the pages of Josiah Gregg's *Commerce of the Prairies* and of Washington Irving's *Captain Bonneville* and *Astoria* had already filled men's minds with dreams of a good land of limitless space. George Catlin's pictures of the Mandan villages along the Missouri had introduced the great plains and their inhabitants to fireside people both in the United States and Europe, and the very newspapers of Jackson's boyhood took on dignity as they told of the emigration to Oregon and the westward passage of the Mormons.

In the year of Jackson's birth, 1843, John Charles Fremont's first published report only half-hid in measured language the proud excitement of the explorer as he described for his countrymen the conquest of the high peaks and the wonders of the Rockies. Indeed, within a few weeks of the birthday of the man who was to be the picture-maker of the West, Fremont was preparing his thirty-nine trappers, scouts and voyageurs at the mouth of the Kansas River for the second and greatest of his expeditions.

As late as the summer of 1840, the last of the Trappers' Rendezvous had been held on Horse Creek of the Green River, and the fabulous Mountain Men had bartered furs, talked tall and held profane holiday as of old.

Deep-burdened covered wagons creaked in endless trains along the Oregon Trail, in the years after 1842. Young Jackson saw them in his mind's eye, winding past Chimney Rock on the North Platte River in western Nebraska.

In order to avoid the bad lands by the river banks, the Trail turned inland and headed over Mitchell's Pass at Scott's Bluff.

Fort Laramie, as a post of the American Fur Company and as a government frontier post, was a way station where the wagon trains refitted after the long drive from the Missouri River. Inside its adobe walls, the emigrants were safe for the moment from the never-ceasing Indian peril.

On the north bank of the Sweetwater River was a landmark of which everyone had heard, Independence Rock, where the wagons pulled up in corral for water and the drivers exchanged information on conditions along the trail. The rock was covered with carved names of those who had come thus far, two-fifths of the way to Fort Vancouver. Through Devil's Gate beyond the rock, the Sweetwater bored through the granite walls of the mountains.

At the southern end of the Wind River Range, South Pass through the Rockies opened out to the weary wagoners, so easily and gradually that in Fremont's words, "the traveller, without being reminded of any change by toilsome ascents, suddenly finds himself on waters which flow to the Pacific Ocean."

Southwestward from the Pass, at the division of the Oregon and Mormon Trails, Jim Bridger, one of the original "mountain men," had built his trading post (shown *below*) in the year of Jackson's birth. For forty-six years he dealt in furs, gave wise advice to emigrants and explorers, was a solicitous husband to three (successive) squaws, and told wild tales of the marvels of the upper Yellowstone region. Everyone came to Fort Bridger: wagon trains with emigrants; missionaries; Indians on foot, on horseback, or dragging their goods on travois.

During the spring of 1860, to young William Henry Jackson, as to all other Americans on farms, in city offices, at the wheels of ships, it was plain that the nation was hurrying to calamity. Yet, on the eve of conflict, all men thrilled as he did at the news of the first run of the Pony Express.

It was easy to fancy the alert rider at full gallop with the mail along the stages between St. Joseph, Missouri, and Sacramento, California. He was a tempting prey for stalking Indians who feared him with a dumb, prophetic dread as the advance man of a new horde of settlers.

The chase past Split Rock, in the valley of the Sweetwater River, would be grim and close, the rider's Colt revolver ready in his hand . . .

... but his spent mount carried him safely to the Relay Station, where the rifles of the Agent and his men covered his approach and dispersed the Indians. Then the *mochilla* was lifted to a fresh horse, and in two minutes the rider was off again for South Pass. These Relay Stations, spaced at fifteen-mile intervals, were ready, day and night, summer and winter, for the work of forwarding the mail.

The *mochilla* was a leather square with four, padlocked pockets in which the mail was carried. It fitted snugly over the saddle; the rider was actually seated on it, his legs between the pockets as he rode.

As the rider left the Relay Station, he was sped on his way by the Agent and by members of a wagon train, presumably refitting for the westward progress.

Men at work on the extension of the telegraph line cheered the passing Pony Express man with unconscious irony. The completion of the transcontinental telegraph in October, 1861, ended all need for the tough little ponies and their fearless, lithe riders.

The Overland Stage had its own dramatic story; one which is kept feebly alive in the tent-shows and rodeos of the present day. In Jackson's time, however, the mail, freight and passenger haul from Atchison, Kansas, to Placerville, California, and to by-points on branch lines, was an economic necessity. South Pass Station (shown *above*), one of ninety-three between Atchison and Salt Lake City, was often raided by Indians.

And on the open plains the stage would race to safety within the corral of wagons an emigrant train had drawn up for its own defense.

Virginia Dale Station (*below*) was a division center of the Overland Stage route, about a hundred miles north and west of Denver. Supplies were stored there for service of the other stations in the division, and it represented what safety and tranquillity there might be along the road. The station was named for the wife of Joseph Alfred Slade, the outlaw-killing chief of the division.

High water, bad roads and Indian hostility might delay the coaches, but Ben Holladay, the stage-coach king, and his tough, loyal drivers bulled it through as best they could and justified the boast that the Overland was "The Great Through Mail Between The Atlantic and Pacific States."

Emigrant trains, Pony Express riders, stage-coach drivers, hostile Indians, all these, and the fierce jollity at the lonesome stations, the ready comradeship of hard-living men, made up William Henry Jackson's dream of the country he was to know so well in a few years' time. It was these scenes he chose to paint when leisure waited on memory.

PEACE IN VERMONT AND WAR IN VIRGINIA

BOYHOOD went swiftly by in the "little red schoolhouse" and on the family farm near Peru, New York. Life was arithmetic, ballgames in summer, his mother's patient lessons in water-color and his own discovery of Chapman's magical *American Drawing Book*. Life was coasting down-hill on the winter snow, and an artist's growing preoccupation with the form and color of things. The talented lad soon had his chance to paint for a living; humble subjects near at hand, portraits of neighbors, show-cards for shopkeepers, political posters for the Presidential campaign of his hero, Fremont, in 1856. The well-remembered schoolhouse!

In 1858, a photographer in Troy, New York, employed Jackson as part-time retoucher and artist. As he washed water-color over the stolid black and white prints, his mind was quick to note every operation that was performed in the studio. The new art of photography fascinated him.

His real chance came just a month after Lincoln's first Presidential victory. Frank Mowrey, of Rutland, Vermont, gave Jackson a steady job as studio artist and became his generous friend and teacher. The self-portrait *above* shows Jackson at seventeen, a happy apprentice to photography.

On his days off he tramped the country about Rutland and drew in his sketchbook a record of the local hills and streams. The sketches on the facing page illustrate the boy's intuitive feeling for what was significant in landscape, an attitude that will be seen as dominant through his later career.

Secession! The flag down on Sumter! Volunteers flocked to the colors, but as the toll of Gaines' Mill, Frayser's Farm and Malvern Hill was taken, the President called for more men. Company K, Twelfth Regiment, Second Vermont Brigade, enlisted young Jackson, and he was set to work on the fortifications near Alexandria, Virginia. (*right*).

Colonel Blunt soon recognized Jackson's special abilities and made him official staff artist. In this capacity, he made maps and recorded camp life around Fairfax Court House.

While the regiment awaited action, Jackson sent home many sketches of "camp types" like the one shown *left*. His army experience was a continual education in life and men, and the possibilities of art.

J. S. FRINK — "SUTLER.."

As the Sixth Corps moved past Jackson's post near the old battlefield of Bull Run on June 15, 1863, the comic-opera soldier shown *right* little thought that he would fight no longer "mit Sigel," but under Sedgwick at Gettysburg.

In winter, soldiering was heroic for William Henry Jackson only as it required heroic endurance of snow and frost in camp and on the dreary rounds of guard duty.

And in warmer weather an occasional wash-day broke the monotony of foraging, hen-roost robbing and map-making.

When his enlistment came to an end in 1863, Jackson took up where he had left off in Rutland. An offer from Styles' "Gallery of Art" in Burlington, Vermont, would not have moved him had not Frank Mowrey pointed out that the opportunity to advance in his profession would be greater in the university town. Styles had a good reputation as an artist, and an establishment more impressive than the average studio of the day. The customers did business in the front office (*left*).

They waited their turns in this Reception Room (*right*), which was hung with samples of photographic art and made comfortable according to the standards of a time of "straight-backs."

A towering "base-burner" heated the studio where the actual photographing was done. Light poured down through the glass roof. The furnishings and background could be altered to suit the sitter's whim, but there was no escaping the vise-like clutch of the head-clamps.

In the day of the big, box-camera and the collodion wet-plate, photography was no occupation for amateurs. Jackson set all his energies toward mastery of a profession which he felt would permit him to be both an artist and a solvent citizen. He made the double self-portrait on a single plate, shown *above*, in 1865.

It is presumed that the group *above* was made up of fellow-members of the SSC (Social Sardine Club to the initiate), a society of young men about town. William Henry Jackson is seen, seated, to the *right*.

DREAM INTO REALITY

AFTER a year of Army life, Vermont seemed dull and changed to young Jackson. The photographer's studio had walls. The old mountains around his home held no challenge. His best girl was too prim. The great West of his boyish dream was the place for young men—the West of the scouts and the high places—Fremont's West! He picked up his tall hat, shook the dust of Vermont from his feet, and fared forth.

By Monday morning, April 16, 1866, the trail had led only as far as New York City, but Fate intervened there in the person of Rock Rounds, an old comrade of Company K. Many a time, around Virginian camp-fires, they had talked of the country across the Mississippi and listened to the yarns of soldier-adventurers who had been there, or said they had. And here was Rock, off to mine silver in Montana! His friend Billy Crowl was weary of counter-jumping at J. B. Claflin's great emporium, and Billy was going too. Why shouldn't W. H. Jackson join them? The mining companies were only too happy to pay the passage of promising young men to the diggings.

On closer inquiry that same day, it appeared that the mining companies had grown less benevolent. There were jobs . . . but they were in Montana. And as the would-be miners were listening with long faces to this piece of information, Jackson clapped his hand to his pocket and found that his wallet was missing and all his ready money with it.

A young man followed his dream hard in 1866. A pawnbroker advanced enough cash on a watch and chain to pay the fare as far as Detroit, and after a two-day railway journey the three of them arrived in that city, broke but trusting in the Western gods. Almost two months of odd jobs and near starvation followed, until they had money enough in hand for passage to the frontier city of St. Joseph, Missouri. An advertisement in the St. Joseph *Morning Herald* brought them the first welcome news they had had since leaving New York. The Intelligence Office on Francis Street was looking for a hundred teamsters to cross the Plains. Twenty dollars a month! Unlimited opportunities for advancement!

On Saturday, June 23, Rock Rounds, Billy Crowl and William Henry Jackson, plug-hatted and brash, walked aboard the river steamer *Denver,* their agency fees paid out of five dollars that Jackson had borrowed from a sympathetic teamster. They were bound for Nebraska City and bullwhacking jobs on a wagon train. Ed Owens would be their future boss.

Profanely pointed comments of other bullwhackers moved the three men to get rid of their toppers as soon as they were able to draw trail equipment against future pay.

Bullwhackers were housed in the blistering sun on the top deck as the *Denver* churned up the Missouri toward Nebraska City. A preponderantly feminine cargo of Mormons held themselves aloof.

Ed Owens, pictured on the facing page, was patient and gentlemanly with his feckless, new hands. Like all Plains wagonmasters, he was dictator absolute on the road; he set the routes, picked camp-sites, and watched over the safety of his twenty-five wagons of valuable cargo, three hundred oxen or "bulls", and the attendant bullwhackers.

Ed. Owens 1866
Wagon Boss - from
Nebraska City -

At five o'clock in the morning, after the night-herder had rounded up the bulls and sent them crowding and bellowing into the corral of wagons, came "Yoking-Up" time.

When the first drive of the day ended at ten in the morning, the bulls were turned out to graze and the bullwhackers greased the wheel-hubs of the wagons. And then the yoking-up job had to be done all over again.

Yoking a Wild "Bull"

Just before sunset, the train halted and made camp; the bulls were set loose; and the men hit the grub pile for bread, bacon and coffee. Unless someone had knocked down game, the menu was invariable.

"The whips they use on the Plains are enormous things made of rawhide, plaited, about twelve feet long or more, an inch and a half in diameter at the belly, and with a stock about eighteen inches to two feet in length," said Jackson in a letter to his people back home.

On June 26, 1866, near Fort Kearny, about a hundred and seventy miles west of Nebraska City, Jackson sketched the corral (*above*) and noted in his diary:

"Our greatest affliction was dust; it was fearful, and sometimes so thick that it was impossible to see more than a single rod. We heard a thousand and one rumors of Indian hostilities. At Kearny, they would not let less than thirty wagons pass and every man was required to be armed."

California Crossing is shown *above*, as Jackson saw it. "Arrived at the crossing place on the South Platte, some two or three miles below Julesburg, July 24th. When we arrived, there were some three or four other trains preparing to cross. We uncoupled our wagons and put from twelve to eighteen yoke to each single wagon. Current so swift, it takes some of the smaller oxen off their feet in the deepest parts. Crossing at the same time were large bands of Sioux . . ."

Heading across to the south side of the North Platte, the wagon train came to Chimney Rock on July 31.

By August 3, the outline of Scott's Bluff had moved in from the horizon. The recently built telegraph line stood close to the trail. As the train creaked out of Mitchell's Pass (*right*), Jackson's team ran away downhill and almost tumbled him into the Bad Lands.

Beyond Fort Laramie (see page 3) a Mormon party was encountered on the Big Bitter Cottonwood. They were caught in one of the vicious thunderstorms common to the North Platte country.

"Along the Sweetwater River [two hundred miles west of Fort Laramie] there was plenty of food for cattle and plenty of buffalo chips for fire. Before any of us are aware of it, we are nearly through the South Pass. The weather was extremely cold in the Pass." Jackson sketched the approach to the Pass (*above*) on August 30, 1866.

From camp on the Little Sandy, September 2, the Wind River Mountains loomed up to the northeast.

The time had come for Jackson to revise a few of his ideas. Rock Rounds had jumped the wagon train to take a job with the telegraph company's construction crew, and that was a pretty clear indication of what Rock thought of their original Montana venture. Perhaps the golden city of San Francisco would be a better objective than the silver mines to the north. Better or no, Jackson made up his mind to head there by way of Salt Lake City. There was little time to lose, for the road to Montana branched off at Ham's Fork; accordingly, Jackson faced up to Ed Owens with the news that he and Billy Crowl were going to quit the train.

The suave wagonmaster lost his temper. His blistering curses and wild threats moved the impressionable Billy to change his mind and stay with the train, but Jackson stood fast by his decision. He walked the few miles to South Bend Stage Station and waited hopefully there for a wagon train bound for the Mormon metropolis. On September 27, 1866, a short-handed outfit came through and hired Jackson at a dollar a day to handle a six-yoke team.

The start of the journey was idyllic. Jackson had leisure enough to sketch a panorama of the Uinta Mountains from Quaking Asp Hill.

A little later on, the train passed beneath the red rock walls of Echo Canyon.

The junction of Echo and Weber Canyons (*below*) was reached without incident. But in Parley's Park, up among the last mountain barriers to the Salt Lake valley, the train ran into a snowstorm and the passage over was achieved knee-deep in mud and snow. The cattle gave out and the drivers hauled the wagons across by main strength.

14 Junction of Echo and Weber Canyons.

On the morning of October 19, the wagons were able to descend into the valley, and Jackson saw the Great Salt Lake, the inland sea.

M & J as he reached Salt Lake in the fall of 1866 —

The sketch to the *right* is Jackson's unflattering view of himself as he entered Salt Lake City. He was almost broke, and his first thought was to get a job. Dreams were poor fare for a hungry belly.

When there appeared to be no demand for an artist or photographer's assistant in Salt Lake City, Jackson went to work on Birch's farm (*above*) as general utility man. Birch and his family were kindly, simple people who had come out to Brigham Young's country from the rural districts of England. South of their farm, the Wasatch Range filled up the whole view.

An occasional trip was made to town with garden truck. There was endless discussion, of evenings in the farm kitchen, and several of the elders tried to convert Jackson to the doctrines of Joseph Smith.

He might have stayed at Birch's farm forever had not a package of presentable clothes and a hundred dollar remittance from his family arrived in December and released him from bread and butter bondage. He made a deal for transport with Ed Webb, who ran a wagon train from Salt Lake to Los Angeles, and after paying his fare and buying necessities for the trip, bade farewell to the Birch family and set off for California. They reached Utah Lake (*above*) on Christmas Day.

Webb's train was travelling light and making good time. On December 27 they passed through the little town of Nephi, Utah (*below*), south of the Lake.

The Old Spanish Trail followed the Virgin River for fifty miles or more, and at the point seen in the sketch *above* was part of the Salt Lake-Los Angeles road across the Great Basin.

Webb's train toiled up out of the Valley of the Virgin (as shown *below*) and headed southwest for the Valley of the Vegas, near the site of the present Boulder Dam.

The Joshua Yuccas towered up, twenty to thirty feet high, as the train bore Jackson through the Mohave Desert. At the desert's western rim was Cajon Pass which would lead him down to Southern California's green land and Los Angeles, his goal.

When he saw Los Angeles on January 31, 1867, it was still a small town (as shown *below*), Spanish in style and tone but Yankee-sharp in trade. He sold his rifle there at a good forty percent loss.

The one little church drowsed in the calm of a Los Angeles Sunday afternoon, but the prevalent peace and quiet did not appeal to Jackson.

When he heard that things were stirring at Clear Creek Mines, he headed north on foot through San Fernando Pass (*below*). He and his companion, Bill Maddern (a fellow-sufferer from gold-fever), stopped for a solid meal at Major Gordon's ranch.

Some ninety miles above Los Angeles a stampeding herd of wild cattle was headed off by Jackson and his friend as shown *above*. It was a close call.

On the edge of the Tehachipi Hills, below the pass that led into the San Joaquin Valley, lay Twenty-Mile Ranch (*below*), a stage station and road house owned by emigrants named Ward who came originally from New York State. Here, Jackson put in a back-breaking time as handy man and official family portraitist. Bill Maddern pushed on, alone, to the mining country.

Toward the end of March, Jackson began to think again of the East and his home. The gold-fever had run its course, and trouble and disappointment had matured the romantic boy into intelligent manhood. It would be wiser to return to his family and his friends.

The Wards were scrupulous to pay him what he had earned. He set off for Los Angeles again, and arriving there on March 30, took counsel with the kindly Ed Webb and his wife. There was a way for a man to work his passage eastward, but it was a hard way.

Half-broken horses, broncos and mustangs, sold for a few dollars in California, but enterprising men could run them to Omaha where their re-sale might bring in as much as two hundred percent profit. Sam McGannigan was such a man, and he was about to start with a drove. Although he side-stepped any discussion of wages, he took Jackson on as an extra hand "just to see how he'd make out".

Between the middle of April and May 3, when Jackson left with the drove, there were lively times on the range outside town, as seen *below*. For, before you could take a drove of wild horses from Los Angeles to Omaha, you had to catch and brand them.

Catching up horses in California - April 1867

From Cocomunga Ranch in San Bernardino Valley, thirty miles or so on their eastward way, there was a fine view of the distant Cajon Pass (*above*).

McGannigan's horse drive was following the same route eastward that Ed Webb had used for the westward journey. The stock was wild and the hands were green, so the pursuit of errant horses was all in the day's work (*right*).

Once through the Cajon Pass, the sands of the Mohave Desert (*below*) reached out to the far mountains. As the dusty, sweaty days succeeded one another, Jackson became more and more disgusted with his job and with the company he was keeping. Sam McGannigan was a bullying coward who alternated between whining and roaring.

Near Cottonwood Springs (*above*) the horses made their daily stampede, and this time the wagons had to be repaired. In the intense heat the animals were restless for water.

Crossing the Sevier River in flood on June 13 had been hard, but no stock had been lost, and Nephi, Utah, was reached on June 15.

In Parley's Canyon (*above*), other groups of eastward travellers were encountered and there was much talk about the Indian raids that might be expected on a small, poorly-manned horse drive.

But the Indians did not appear, and the Fourth of July was celebrated within sight of Bridger Butte, (*below*), three miles east of Fort Bridger on Black's Fork of the Green River. Within a few miles of this spot had been held the Trappers' Rendezvous of earlier days. (See page 1).

Swimming Green River —

The Green River was in flood when the drive reached it on July 9 at noon. After several attempts to swim the horses across (*above*), Sam McGannigan gave it up and the stock was ferried over. The thought of this expense preyed on Sam's mind, and when the party made camp at Medicine Bow, Wyoming, he went on a two-day drunk to forget.

From Fort Sanders to Julesburg, other trains joined up for mutual aid in the event of Indian attacks. The commandant of the Fort gave them an armed guard, and they met small detachments of Pawnee scouts all along the way. The Cheyenne and Sioux were active, and a line of burned buildings and new graves along Lodge Pole Creek supplied visual proof.

The Union Pacific Railroad was pushing hardily ahead. Jackson saw the construction crews a few miles east of Fort Sanders, in the Laramie Hills. The tie-cutters and graders were out in front, and the rail-layers a long breath behind them, working under protection of United States troopers.

The drive ended on July 30 at Julesburg, in 1867 the western terminus of the Union Pacific. Stock and handlers were crammed together into box cars for the thirty-six hour run to Omaha, where the horses were corralled and Jackson made up his mind to demand a financial reckoning of Sam.

RAILS HEADING WEST

ACKSON stood on the road that ran past the miry bottom lands where Sam McGannigan had pitched the horse camp. Omaha lay two or three miles to the south. It was Tuesday, August 6, 1867, and he had just finished his last interview with Sam. Twenty dollars for three months' wages, and at that grudgingly given! Twenty dollars for the heat of the Mohave Desert; for hours in icy streams on fruitless attempts to save ferry charges! Five times twenty dollars would have been little enough for putting up with Sam's company during the drive.

The western dream seemed to have disappeared. The free life of adventure exacted a hard price from a man. Cold and rags and hunger were realities. Frozen feet and boils from bad food were realities. There were no longer any comfortable prospects back East; for now that he was halfway home he knew that pride would ever block the path of his return until he had something to show in the way of success.

Unlimited opportunities! That echo from the days in St. Joe was hollow. He had a pocketful of sketches and a dirty twenty-dollar bill to show for sixteen months of hard labor. He picked up his bag, looked about him and began to trudge toward town. There would be nothing for him in the huddle of small houses and shops, litter, railroad men and Indians that was Omaha in the fall of 1867. He would thank Omaha for the chance to buy a haircut, a shave and a new suit.

As the slap-slap of the barber's brush and the light touch of the razor soothed him, some of the anger and bitterness began to drain away; the sight of his bright, barbered face in the mirror of the clothes shop, and the feel of clean, new clothes completed the cure. The barber had told him there were two photographers in town, and that sounded like good business. Besides, Sam McGannigan was not the whole human race. The world was full of good, helpful people; like Frank Mowrey who had taught him his trade, Bill Maddern the merry companion of the California trails, and the long, silent teamster who had loaned him the agency fee in St. Joseph. There would be men like these in Omaha. And he had health, and a profession, and the Yankee conviction that hard, good work always paid off. More than all this, he had seen the mountains, the high places, and in them sensed a vocation. The West was a new reality; it was no longer a dream. One day he would conquer the high places with lens and wet-plate.

Of the two photographers in town one was a canny, timorous soul, but Hamilton, the other, was willing to take a chance on an unknown quantity in a new suit. Jackson soon struck a satisfactory bargain with him. There was plenty of business. In a short time Jackson was managing a branch of Hamilton's shop on shares, and before eight months were up he had bought out his employer and the canny competitor, too.

During those busy months he regained his belief in himself, and he began to discover something of the rapidly growing city as he met the people of Omaha on the streets and in his studio. It was a friendly, lively city and had been so ever since 1863 when it had taken heart of grace with the westward push of the Union Pacific Railroad and had seen its destiny as eastern terminus of that mighty enterprise.

The big boom had come in 1866, and now in 1868 an acrid dispute was on as to whether the proposed railroad bridge across the Missouri River was an accommodation for Council Bluffs or a chance for the trains to terminate in a *real* city. The businessmen and the shopkeepers were proud of their establishments. They liked to have pictures made of them in this time of their two-story infancy, so that they might point with pride in the years when they would rival the shops of Chicago and New York. Omaha had come a long way since the days of 1854 when the town had been three houses and a "soddy" saloon; when the boys among the corralled wagons sang,

> *"I'm a bullwhacker, far from my home,*
> *If you don't like me, just leave me alone;*
> *Eat my grub when hungry, drink when dry,*
> *Whack, punch, swear, then lie down and die"*

and then strolled to the riverside where Elder Shinn kept the ferry by day and preached in his little tabernacle by night. A fine, ribald obbligato they would set up to his sound, Methodist doctrine until the witty and wily old man matched them and talked them down, or until someone impressed by his good humor and sincerity called out:

"He runs a fair ferry, boys. Give him a chance."

And in those days Editor J. W. Pattison of the *Omaha Arrow*, sitting in the tent he somewhat ostentatiously called his "editorial sanctum," could write with real prophesy that, "one day the busy hum of Omaha factories, the incessant rattle of drays over paved streets, the steady tread of thousands of men" would fill the Nebraska air. It was journalism in the tradition of Mark Twain's fabulous western editors, but his prophesy had taken only fifteen years to come true. In the year Jackson set up his business in Omaha, Brownell Hall, "an elegant young ladies' seminary," had opened at Jones Street and 16th, and its very existence was witness of a basic change in values. Omaha was aspiring.

Even if the legislature had moved to the new capitol at Lincoln, the eminence from which this bird's-eye view of the city was taken still carried the name of "Capitol Hill."

A horse-car moved along rails in the center of the muddy street. Two-horse rigs from the surrounding farms had brought their owners in to shop. F. A. Schneider's hardware store on the right-hand side of the street was run by one of the first settlers.

Will R. King's grocery, halfway down on the right-hand side, was new in 1868. His old store on Farnam and 12th Streets had been the scene of a gruesome murder. Higgins, his cashier, was putting away the receipts on the night of November 21, 1866, when Baker, the porter, killed him with an axe and stole the money. Baker was tried and hanged, the second man to suffer legal execution in the community. Eight thousand people witnessed the execution, when it took place on the High School grounds, and were edified at Baker's complete, public confession.

Milton Rogers occupied the corner store in the principal business block. He had begun as a tinsmith in a cottonwood-log shack at Council Bluffs, and he had opened the Omaha branch of his stove trade in 1855. This Farnam Street store and the block in which it was located were built by him in 1868 and are an index of the popularity of the "Crown Jewel" base-burner in which he dealt. He was a man of vision, too, and put a dollar or two in the South Omaha stock-yards.

James K. Ish, whose wholesale drug-store adjoined Rogers's, began business in 1856 and with rare foresight brought with him the lumber for his first shop and a pair of carpenters to put it up.

W. P. Wilcox, of Stephens and Wilcox, dry-goods, had been one of the old-time Missouri River steamboat captains until he retired to trade. Farther down Farnam Street, and out of our sight, stood McDonald's Ladies' Emporium of Fashion, which was in the words of the proprietor, "to Omaha what Worth's was to Paris: a place where the form is fitted and the eye is pleased."

The first hotel in Omaha was the Douglas House, built in 1855. The Herndon House was erected in 1857 and was designed to be the "best hotel west of Chicago." Despite the patronage of Omaha's best people, it slipped down the scale and was taken over at last by the Union Pacific for a headquarters.

The Metropolitan at 12th and Douglas Street, shown to the *left*, catered to drummers and transients, set a good table, was unpretentious, and prospered.

This is the Cozzens Hotel. It cost $40,000.00 and was built in two months' time by George Francis Train in order to soothe his outraged nerves. As he was dining one evening at the Herndon House in the days of its decline, the wind blew in on him through a broken window with such force that he was obliged to hire a man to stand between him and the draft until he had finished his meal. This experience convinced him that Omaha needed a good, new hotel, and before he laid his head on his pillow that night, he had planned and contracted for the Cozzens Hotel.

In 1869 the true symbol of Omaha was the railroad and all things connected with it. The blacksmith's shop, shown to the *right*, was only a tiny unit of the huge engineering and commissary organization needed for construction of the eastern section of the transcontinental span.

Under the forceful leadership of General Grenville Dodge, the Union Pacific drove across the plains toward the great divide; for every mile of track laid, Congress offered at first 6,400 acres of public land, and later twice that much, plus a cash subsidy that varied with the difficulty of the terrain. The Central Pacific was moving eastward from San Francisco at a far better rate of speed, and was empowered by Act of Congress in 1866 to push past its original terminus at the California-Nevada line and make connection with the lagging Union Pacific wherever fate and energy of construction might decide.

With so much public land and cash subsidy at stake, the pace of building became almost inhuman, and the war-tautened nerves of the nation thrilled again to a fight as the railheads raced toward each other.

Early in 1869 exhausted directors of both companies called time, and Promontory Point, Utah, was agreed upon as the place where the two roads would meet. A motley crowd of tracklayers, politicians, soldiers and Indians looked on as Leland Stanford, President of the Central Pacific, drove the last, golden spike into the final tie, and the locomotives "119" and "Juniper" touched cowcatchers in the final act of the drama.

While events were moving toward this end, Jackson was not so absorbed in getting a new business underway that he neglected the relation of these happenings to himself. Living as he was in a great moment of history, he sought for some way in which he might take a part. In years to come, people were going to marvel at this bridge over a continent and ask in what way it was done. Conscious of the untried possibilities of photography, he resolved to go out along the road and make pictures of the final stages of construction. It would be a reasonable business venture as well, for the vogue of stereoscopic "viewing" was well on, and the comfortable people back East liked to share vicariously in the hardships and excitements of trail-breaking. He prepared special travelling equipment; packed the whole affair in a wooden box that was carry-all, darkroom and studio; and set off westward from Omaha.

The railroad had shifted the traditional road across the prairies from the south side of the River Platte to the north side, in order to escape the periodical floods and soft ground. At the forks of the river, where the town of North Platte had come into being, rough-hewn logs supported the bridge across the north branch (*above*).

This country had been Sioux country once. Jackson was reminded of the savage fights only a year or two before, when Pawnee scouts under Major North had defended the grading operations beyond Ogallala and Julesburg against raiding Cheyenne and Sioux. Some of the men in that famous fighting unit had posed for him in his Omaha studio.

White Horse was proud of his uniform, and he used tomahawk and revolver with equal skill. His scalp-lock challenged his enemies to "come and get it."

Reading from *left* to *right*, you may see Blue Hawk and his companion, Coming-Around-With-The-Herd, both of the Pawnee scouts.

Rattlesnake, shown *above,* was an old acquaintance. When McGannigan's horse drive had encountered the Pawnee scouts along Lodge Pole Creek, back in '67, this Indian had commanded the detachment which escorted them to Julesburg.

When in 1866 a dispute over the theft of a buffalo-meat cache broke out between the Skidi Pawnees and the Kitkehahki, or Republican Pawnees, Sky Chief (*above*) met with Major North in an effort to prevent war. Sky Chief is pictured wearing a medal commemorative of his share in a council with government representatives. He died at Massacre Canyon in 1873, fighting against the Sioux.

Eagle Chief, shown *above,* shared in the negotiations over the stolen cache. Major North decided that the Kitkehahki families who had suffered from the loss of the meat should be indemnified by the Skidis, but that neither tribe should be considered to have lost face in the process.

When Jackson reached Cheyenne, Wyoming, the two-year-old railroad town had become an important division point on the Union Pacific, but it had kept much of the "boom town" atmosphere of 1867. The street scene to the *left* was one of several Jackson made for local merchants, the while he prepared for his trips along the line.

He met Doctor F. V. Hayden again in Cheyenne, and renewed a casual Omaha acquaintance which was to influence his entire career.

West of Cheyenne, he set up his portable studio near the bed of Dale Creek and took a picture of the bridge from below. The calico hood over the box had holes in it just large enough to admit his head and hands. Under this hood he prepared his plates and developed them after exposure.

Above is another view of Dale Creek Bridge. Near Green River Station, Wyoming,
Jackson photographed Green River Butte, as seen *below*.

This photograph of Petrified Fish Cut, also in the neighborhood of Green River Station, is still remarkable for its magnificent clarity and the detail of rock formations shown in it. This view and the one just preceding it were to have decisive influence on the course of Jackson's career and were to give him an opportunity to satisfy all his ambitions.

But that happy time of fulfillment was almost a year in the future. Meanwhile he set up his tent in Echo Canyon beside the railroad tracks, traded pictures of train crews for free rides from place to place, and waited in bad weather for chemicals to be sent him from Salt Lake City.

Evenings under canvas were times for dreaming, despite the ants and cockroaches that made sleep a hazard. This expanding West was going to be greater than anyone suspected. He, William Henry Jackson, was ready and able to record its story. Later on, when it became dull and settled and familiar, there would be new frontiers.

It is easy to see from the lay and grading of the tracks at the head of Echo Canyon, shown *above*, why the major part of the line had to be re-laid after the race for Promontory Point and the collapse of the first boom in Union Pacific securities. The trestle work in Echo Canyon (*below*) had only recently been finished.

Pulpit Rock (*right*), at the mouth of Echo Canyon, was a well-known landmark and a challenge to climbers.

Three miles beyond the mouth of Echo, the "Amphitheatre" (*below*) towered in a huge, semicircular mass, better than a thousand feet above the tracks and the telegraph.

Jackson made his way about on work-trains like this one, trading off pictures for his fare and for food from the railroad hash-houses. In the construction camps he visited, "work, drink and fight" was the order of the day among the random jumble of nationalities who were "working on the railroad."

At Devil's Gate Bridge over the Weber River, in northern Utah, the Union Pacific entered the Wasatch country. The debris of construction lay raw over what had been solemn and lonely mountains.

As the railroad ground its way westward, tunnels scarred the Wasatch rocks, untouched since Miocene times.

The rock formation in Weber Canyon (shown *left*) was named the "Devil's Slide." A generation of men, Mormons and railroaders alike, who had striven mightily with the manifestations of Old Nick in these mountains, were fond of attaching his name to familiar places.

Westward down the valley from Tunnel Number Four was a stretch of track that must have pleased the pick and shovel men after their experiences tunnelling through the Wasatch.

The only way Jackson could replenish his outfit of chemicals and papers, at this point almost exhausted, was to make a special trip by Wells, Fargo stage to Salt Lake City where Savage and Ottinger's studio might help him out . . . at a price.

He took time, while in the City, to see Annie Ward play in a piece whose title he did not record. The old Salt Lake City theatre is shown to the *left*. Unlike many other reforming gentlemen, Brigham Young saw no harm in stage plays and had a special box at the theatre.

But the Union Pacific main line did not go through Salt Lake City. Instead it turned northward around the Lake and passed through the hopeful tent city of Corinne.

While trains lay over for a short while here, the staff of the "Daily Reporter" would rush through a special souvenir edition containing the names of the passengers —and sell it out every time.

As traffic developed, Corinne grew into the metropolis shown *above*. Presumably, the only reason some member of the firm of Platt and Russel was not visible in his doorway was his absence elsewhere on a painting job. John Kupfer's shop housed a hardware store and a gunsmith in addition to the proprietor's jewelry business. But fate willed that a city named Brigham should prosper and Corinne should fail to thrive.

At the other end of Corinne's Main Street was the Uintah House, which charged a dollar for dinner.

Near Corinne, the lone tree shown *right* was another familiar landmark. It marked a distance of exactly one thousand railroad miles from Omaha.

The picture of Promontory Point, Utah (*below*), was taken two months after the driving of the golden spike. The flag marks the point where on May 10, 1869, the Union Pacific and Central Pacific lines were joined. In the words of Bret Harte's poem on the occasion:

"What was it the Engines said,
Pilots touching, head to head?
Said the Union, 'Don't reflect, or
I'll run over some Director.'
Said the Central, 'I'm Pacific,
But when riled I'm quite terrific.
Yet, today we shall not quarrel,
Just to show these folks this moral:
How two Engines, in their vision,
Once have met without collision.'
That is what the Engines said,
Unreported and unread;
Spoken slightly through the nose,
With a whistle at the close."

The weather grew hotter and more sultry as the summer of 1869 progressed, and a haze settled down over the canyon country which made photography difficult. Clouds of dust blew through Jackson's tent and sifted into his equipment as he tried to develop what pictures he was able to take. No matter how his eye might delight in the varying compositions and color contrasts the unsettled weather provided for him, the limitations of his camera were only too well known to him. He was obliged to live by his wits again, for no money came from Omaha and the commissions he was able to pick up in Corinne and the railroad camps provided just enough cash for absolute necessities. But casting up accounts, he felt he had not wasted his time; he was bringing back to Omaha what he knew to be the best pictures of the West ever made.

The trip home was uneventful. At Wasatch, entering the town early in the morning, the first thing he saw was the body of a negro hanging from a telegraph pole. The man had stolen a little money, and fifteen or twenty of the inhabitants had coursed him like a hare, firing after him as he ran. When he was dead, they had hanged him up as an example. A little further on, at Bear River, he met a squaw man, "Indian Bill," who had lived most of his life with Washakie's Shoshones, and for the first time Jackson learned something of this famous chief whom he was soon to meet.

His absence had not been good for business at the Omaha studio, and his first days back there were spent in pulling loose ends together, paying bills and drumming up trade. And all that time, he was wistful for a way of life which would keep him out of cities and among the high peaks. He had come to a few conclusions about mountains. In their majesty and loneliness they were like great men, each with its own personality and moods that varied from hour to hour. They should be pictured, not full-on like prosaic, old Uncle Rupert with his head caught fast in the clamp, but lovingly and respectfully from angles wherein their beauty and changeableness were best displayed. Photography wasn't proper timing and careful chemistry only; the artist's eye had a place, and every moment since his boyhood he had been preparing himself in accuracy and delicacy of vision to be the biographer of these mighty rocks.

Unhappily, these dreams would have to wait. Omaha wedding parties, the opening of new shops, formal portraits in stiff, black clothes of ceremony, were varied in their monotony by curious, proud Indians who waited outside the studio until he lured them in to pose for him. Several of the Indian studies he did were of famous men among the Pawnees.

Among the Indians photographed were Night Chief (*seated*) and Man-Who-Left-His-Enemy-Lying-In-Water (*standing*). The latter of these had won fame for a dash on pony-back through thirty Sioux warriors during the Muddy Creek fight in 1868. Although he holds a gun in this picture, he was famous for his orange-wood bow, a perfect specimen of bow-making, which was said to have been strong enough to send an arrow clear through a buffalo.

Both men are in Pawnee fighting trim, stripped to the waist so that an entering bullet or arrow could not carry cloth into the wound.

Man-Who-Left-His-Enemy-Lying-In-Water appears at the extreme left of the picture to the *right*. Night Chief sits next to him. Then come One-Who-Strikes-The-Chiefs, a celebrated war leader, and Sky Chief, who was photographed earlier by Jackson (see page 52). The warriors are wearing medals presumably commemorative of their part in treaty negotiations with government agents. Peering over their shoulders is Baptiste Bayhalle, half-breed interpreter and scout, whose Indian name meant One-Whom-The-Great-Spirit-Shines-Upon.

Pictured holding the badge of authority, the wing of an eagle, was this old Pitaheue-rat chieftain, Tar-ra-re-caw-wah, reputed to be one of the wisest and most prominent men in his tribe.

A few years after this picture was taken, he died rather mysteriously; it is believed that his resolute opposition to the removal of his people from Nebraska hastened his death.

The travelling dark-room shown *below* was devised by Jackson for his excursions north of Omaha in search of studies made under normal conditions of Indian life.

The Omaha Indian Agency (*above*) at Blair, Nebraska, was under the direction of Dr. Edward Painter, a humanitarian who believed that his charges could be educated and their standard of life raised without eliminating the majority of them or cheating them of what was theirs.

The picture *below* shows the pupils of the Omaha Reservation School assembled on the steps of their school building. Dr. Painter is seen to the left of the group, wearing a broad-brimmed hat.

In addition to his official duties, Dr. Painter soon became a peacemaker between tribal factions, an instructor in scientific farming, and a physician to the bodily ills of any wandering tribesman who called at the back-door clinic he ran in his Agency home. Mrs. Painter is giving food to a squaw while the Indian is having his pulse taken. The girl in the checked dress watering the flowers is Dr. Painter's daughter, Emilie.

The girl sitting her pony side-saddle is Emilie Painter. The others in the group were not identified by Jackson.

Out on the Reservation, Dr. Painter was a welcome guest in the tepees of the tribe. The blanketed Indian on the end holds firmly to his bow, and the grounded gun of the standing figure next to Dr. Painter indicates that the Omaha had not carried regeneration to the point of folly.

This Omaha chief, Gihega, wears a curious headdress for an Indian of the Plains. The Omaha were close allies of the Pawnees, and fought beside them against Cheyenne and Sioux.

The word "Omaha" in Indian language meant "going against the current". The name was prophetic of the fate of the children of the prairie, when they tried to oppose the onrush of land-hungry white men. Where the Indian had followed the thundering herds of buffalo, the green spikes of growing crops signaled the death of one economy and the beginnings of another.

Journeying to Loup Fork, Nebraska, north of Grand Island, Jackson photographed a gathering of Pawnee chiefs assembled for a Council at the Agency. *Left* to *right,* they are: Sun Chief; A-Fine-Horse; Lone Chief; One-Aimed-At; and Struck-With-A-Tomahawk.

This picture of a Plains tepee, in its fine detail and sharpness of image is typical of the skill with which Jackson used his cumbersome equipment, far from his studio and its refinements.

A group of Pawnees are seen *above,* photographed outside an earth lodge, but Jackson did not identify each one in this picture as was his usual custom.

Earth houses were erected by placing heavy posts in a circle and fitting cross-beams into forks at their tops. Poles were then extended in toward a center post; brush was laid over the poles, and earth was piled on the brush. A tunnel-like entrance was left open.

After the removal of the Pawnees from Loup Fork in 1876, the last traces of these ancient homes were ploughed under.

Peta-la-sha-ra (*above*) was one of the most celebrated of the Pawnee chiefs. In 1825 he had been a delegate from his tribe to Washington and succeeded his father, Old Knife, as head of the Chaui band. He died in 1874, strenuously opposing any violation of the Table Creek treaty, to which his had been the first Indian signature.

His son and successor as head of the Chaui was Sun Chief, shown *above*, wearing his President Buchanan medal of 1857. Ironically enough, this medal celebrated the Table Creek treaty between the United States and the Pawnee, which was broken in 1876.

Other authorities say that this is a picture of Pahoo-ka-ta-wah, or Wolves-In-Pools-Of-Water, chief of the Skidirari clan, who died at Loup Fork before the Pawnees left for Oklahoma.

The view *above* of a group of Pawnee earth lodges at Loup Fork shows details of construction, and by comparison with the human figures, some idea of the size of the mounds.

This tribal assembly in the village was held to witness some occasion of great importance; possibly a naming ceremony in which some brave had earned by conspicuous valor the right to assume a name of greater honor.

RUTS OF THE WAGON WHEELS

TOWARD the end of a sultry day, early in July, 1870, William Henry Jackson was taking a breathing spell in his Omaha studio, when the street door-bell clanged to announce a customer. He recognized the bearded, nervous visitor at once. It was the man from the General Land Office, Hayden, whom he had met at Cheyenne in 1869. After the minimum of polite commonplaces, as was his way, Hayden plunged into business.

The primitive's instinct for truth in nicknames had led the Sioux to call this apparently dreamy and diffident scientist "Man Who Picks Up Stones Running." Determination and drive had carried him from the teacher's desk in a one-room country schoolhouse through Oberlin College, to a doctor's degree at Albany Medical School, to a lieutenant-colonel's commission as surgeon with the Union Army during the war, and now to the chair of geology at the University of Pennsylvania. But there was more to Ferdinand Vandiveer Hayden than push and will-power.

Long before the Civil War, some inner compulsion beyond scientific curiosity had driven him from what might have been a quiet, comfortable medical practice to fossil hunts through Montana and South Dakota, and one-man exploring expeditions as far as Fort Benton near the head of navigation on the Missouri River. Armed only with a geologist's hammer, he had lived off the land, walking when he had to, riding when a chance meeting with trappers or hunters gave him the opportunity. He had served as official geologist on the government expeditions of Warren and Raynolds between 1856 and 1859, observing and studying the Dakota Territory and the courses of the Yellowstone, Madison and Gallatin Rivers.

After four years with the Army, he resumed his restless explorations, returning to South Dakota in 1866, and in 1867 travelling through Nebraska. These scientific tours had won him an appointment to directorship of what was later called the "Geological and Geographical Survey of the Territories," a project of the Department of the Interior now famous as the "Hayden Surveys." He had just completed in Omaha the organization and outfitting of the first of these, and was on his way to Cheyenne with the word to march, when Jackson's sign stirred his memory.

He outlined to Jackson in his precise way his proposal to make scientific studies of the new West which the rush of miners, settlers and adventurers had revealed. Earlier myths, like that of the Great American Desert, had had long lives; he intended to prevent future misconceptions by providing the people of the United States with a cold recital of facts about the new domain. But like all men of imagination, his hopes ran beyond the letter of his commission. He dreamed of a vast public province, protected from cynical exploitation and exhaustion by a few, and preserved in beauty for the worthy many. As events were to prove, he was not alone in this way of thinking. William Clagett and the men of the Washburn-Langford party were at one with him, at least in intention. Like him, they remembered the lost woods of the Eastern mountains that had been eaten up by the hungry sawmills, the polluted rivers of the first frontier, the pall of industrial smoke that hung over unquiet cities.

Hayden had arrived at an important truth. Words were impotent to describe in Washington what might be seen in Wyoming. Sketches were always open to charges of exaggeration and unreality. Men in the easy atmosphere of the capital leafed through reports and scientific monographs, if they read them at all, and forgot at the first challenge of interest or prejudice the truths contained in them. If the new art of the camera were capable of greater things than the perpetuation of foolish faces, it might present to Congress a picture of the virgin West that could hardly be disputed. What did Jackson think?

Trembling with excitement, Jackson pulled down his 1869 portfolio. He knew that these were the best photographs ever to have come out of the West; but would Hayden appreciate them, or understand the difficulties under which they had been produced. He tried to explain, but Hayden waved him away.

The scientist turned over picture after picture.

"You can make a picture like this?" he cried, bringing his hand down on a view of rock formations near the Green River Station, "I wouldn't have believed it. Why I could classify the strata from this."

"I can do better," Jackson's natural modesty vanished in the warm flood of praise. "With better equipment . . ."

"We leave Cheyenne next week." Hayden turned suddenly, his eyes snapping with eagerness. "You must come. I can give you nothing but your keep and your kit, but you understand my purpose, and you can make it yours."

Common sense returned, despite the power of those eager, hypnotic eyes. Unpaid bills, the upset condition of his newly established business! Another trip would be folly. Jackson shook his head regretfully.

"I'm sorry . . ."

"Listen to me," Hayden said.

Six days later, as Jackson climbed aboard the train at Omaha laden with the result of a feverish hunt for photographic supplies and general equipment, he wondered whether this sketchy connection with a great government enterprise would be really the way to fulfillment of his dreams of fame and status, or perhaps only a quick jump into bankruptcy. Hayden's handclasp at Cheyenne settled his doubts. Bankrupt or not, he would never regret this association. Something of Hayden's own scientific fire and poetic vision had communicated itself to him.

They would follow the Oregon Trail out to Fort Bridger and return along the Overland Stage Route, Hayden said. The ruts of the wagon trains, thought Jackson happily! How the world moved! He had gone that road as bullwhacker, as tramp photographer, and now . . . scientist.

He took a picture of the Survey under canvas near Cheyenne as a tryout of his camera and new field equipment (*below*).

Transportation was the task of the eternal Army mule. Crop-eared "Hypo" in the center of the group *below* carried the dark-box and bath-holder in one parfleche (a painted-rawhide envelope with loops to hang over the pack saddle), and in the other the camera, plates and chemicals. The tripod and a keg of water for plate washing were lashed between the parfleches.

The expedition broke camp on the morning of August 7, 1870, and set off up Lodge Pole Creek in a cold rain. After a week's march, they reached game country along La Bonté Creek (*above*), in the vicinity of Fort Laramie. One of the party killed an elk and it was quartered and packed for food.

Fort Laramie (*below*) was relatively quiet in late August, 1870. Red Cloud, the brooding Sioux chieftain, and his head men had been taken on a junket to Washington in the hope that a sight of the power and wealth of the Great White Father would quiet their clamor for the Sioux Agency to be located at the Fort rather than in South Dakota. War was the unspoken alternative.

In Converse County, Wyoming, nineteen miles from La Bonté Creek, this natural bridge in La Prele Canyon was discovered and photographed.

The camp scene *below* was made within sight of Red Buttes. The expedition crossed the North Platte near the present location of Casper, Wyoming, a town named (with an incidental misspelling) for Lt. Caspar Collins.

Five years before, at seven o'clock in the morning, July 26, 1865, Lt. Collins had crossed Platte Bridge in command of twenty-five troopers, under orders to relieve a wagon train ambushed by the Sioux. He knew the strength of the hostiles who lay in wait on the north side of the river and the overwhelming odds against the success of his mission. He gave his cap to a friend for a remembrance of him, mounted his horse and led his little troop into the fight. Three-quarters of his men made their way back to the fort at the bridge, but Lt. Collins was one of those who fell.

This small canyon, discovered by Jackson near Casper, was given his name in Hayden's report to Washington. Later known locally as "Sheep Canyon," its original name was restored in 1927 at a formal ceremony.

The Red Buttes provided a background for the picture of Bessemer Bend shown *above*. Here, the Oregon Trail left the North Platte for the Sweetwater Valley.

The wagons used by the Survey and the four-mule teams that hauled them may be clearly seen.

Camp was pitched again, thirty-eight miles farther along the Trail, at the familiar spot *above,* where Independence Rock reared itself two hundred feet above the level valley of the Sweetwater.

Jackson led "Hypo" up the gradual slope on the far side of the Rock and so was able to picture the view shown *below,* looking eastward from the summit. This river had been known as "Sweetwater" ever since the days of Ashley's fur expeditions. It was said that the trappers gave it its name because of its contrast with other brackish streams in the vicinity. The French voyageurs called it "Eau Sucrée," and traced its name to the time a pack mule, laden with sugar, had been lost in it.

Devil's Gate was a tremendous rift in the granite ridge, five miles from Independence Rock, through which the Sweetwater River flowed from one lovely valley, teeming with antelope and buffalo, into another equally lovely.

The route continued along the Sweetwater until the road dipped through a canyon, about thirty-six miles west of Devil's Gate, and crossed the river three times in a short space. This circumstance had given its name to Three Crossings Stage Station, whose ruins are seen in the picture *below*.

Because of continuous Indian trouble, this Station had been abandoned after 1862, and the regular route of the Overland Stages had been moved southward to a safer place.

The camp of the Survey may be seen in the middle distance.

Near the abandoned Station was this grave of a United States soldier, killed at Three Crossings during the Indian raids in April, 1862. Washakie and his Shoshones were accused of these operations against the line of the Overland Stages between Fort Laramie and Green River, but that wily chief established his innocence. Later on, it appeared that the attacks were the work of wandering hostiles from several tribes under the leadership of renegade whites.

The Survey pushed on toward South Pass, making slow time because of the extensive investigations which the geology and topography of the region required.

At Camp Stambaugh, the United States post on the crest of the divide, they came upon seventy lodges of Shoshones encamped near the fort (*below*).

OLD Washakie himself was with his people, and he consented very amiably to pose for his portrait. Jackson caught a great deal of the chieftain's character in the picture on the facing page.

This tall, powerful and politic old Indian was of mixed Shoshone and Umatilla blood. He was born about the beginning of the Nineteenth Century and became chief of the eastern band of the Shoshones around 1844. He succeeded in uniting the scattered groups of his people into a compact political and military instrument. His personal skill, as hunter, strategist and trainer of warriors, gave him a unique dictatorship over the tribe that lasted until his death in 1900. On one of the occasions when the restless young bloods of the tribe threatened his headship, he left the council without a word and returned to it at its next meeting, bearing six enemy scalps which he had taken in single combat on the warpath.

Early in his career he sensed the futility of opposing the whites by force of arms. By his ready aid to emigrants, his friendly relations with the early trappers and adventurers, and by much valuable assistance given the United States Army in its difficult task of tranquillizing the Cheyenne and Sioux, he put himself and his tribe in a very favorable light with the conquerors. A treaty signed at Fort Bridger on July 3, 1868 (about two years before the date of this picture), had guaranteed possession of the Wind River Mountain country to the Shoshones for their reservation, in exchange for their former home in the Green River Valley.

1870

Because of Washakie's readiness to pose, Jackson had no trouble persuading the superstitious Shoshones to follow the chief's example. The foremost tepee is the War Chief's lodge.

A group of squaws and a papoose are seen inside the lodge of "Indian Dick," possibly that son of the chief who was known as Dick Washakie and succeeded his father as head man of the tribe. The papoose is securely laced down on a cradle or carrying-board.

The halt in South Pass allowed some time for swapping yarns. The first, feverish press of activity which Hayden, anxious for the success of his Survey, had exacted from his men was beginning to relax. The campers compared experiences, and all the old, romantic tales were told and retold.

This part of the country was full of the past. Jedediah Smith, that frontier knight-errant who trusted equally his Bible and his rifle, had travelled here in the trapper days. Thomas Fitzpatrick was credited with effective discovery of the Pass in 1824 as he made his returning way from a winter among the Crows, but there were those who said that the party from Astoria under Stuart had come through it in 1812. Bonneville had taken wagons across South Pass in 1832. And so it went.

Some of the men knew the story of Hugh Glass and his fight with the grizzly bear, and others swore to the truth of Mike Fink's wonderful marksmanship, and all had heard tell of the lies of John Colter who claimed he had stumbled over a "hell" of boiling springs and tall, steaming spouts of water at the forks of the Stinkingwater River. Though Colter was almost sixty years dead, Jim Bridger still swore to the truth of it all. But then Jim was author of that wonderful tale of the time Indians had chased him up a narrow canyon, closed at its head by a waterfall two hundred feet high. "And how did you escape them, Jim?" "I didn't. They got my scalp."

The Survey made a two-day trip northward into the Wind River Mountains where, in 1842, Fremont had stood at the summit of the range and been poet enough to write of a bee that buzzed about his head as "a little pioneer of civilization's advance." Fremont's Peak brooded over the lesser mountains.

The party returned from the Wind River country to the familiar Oregon-Mormon Trail which now bore southwest. They crossed the dry, sandy wastes between South Pass and the Green River in almost overpowering heat. The picture *above* shows the Bad Lands of Wyoming at Black's Fork.

Twelve miles further on, the remarkable formation known as Church Buttes was studied and photographed. In the vicinity shown *below*, Hayden collected a wagon-load of fossil fish, relics of the inland sea that once covered the region.

A base was set up at Fort Bridger for the work that was to be done in and about the Uinta Mountains. Jackson's equipment had seen hard service, and while the post carpenter was making him a new dark-box, he journeyed down to Salt Lake City for additional chemicals. A street view in Salt Lake City is shown *left*.

He found time to renew acquaintance with the Utah landmarks, like "The Great Eastern" in Echo Canyon, seen *below*.

"Monument Rock" in Echo Canyon   Ogden Canyon in Weber County

On his return to the Survey's base at Fort Bridger, Jackson joined a party for a trip southward into the Uintas. Judge Carter, the post trader, guided them. On September 17 they camped near an old sawmill. Jackson was able to make some good photographs of the place.

The campers took time for a little relaxation.

But before they looked out on this panorama of the Uintas, they had to hack out a trail up a long ridge through aspen and jack-pine.

From Fort Bridger, the Survey packed up and journeyed to the head of Black's Fork; thence down Henry's Fork to the Flaming Gorge (*above*) on Green River, a glory of bright red rock, which was the first of the canyons navigated by Major John Wesley Powell on his tumultuous trip down the Green and Colorado Rivers in 1869.

Back at Green River Station on the Union Pacific, Jackson photographed the "Giant's Club" . . .

. . . and "Teapot Rock" (*above*), before the expedition set off eastward along the Overland Stage Route through southern Wyoming. This was a cold, drab journey that presented no opportunities for Jackson's camera.

At Fort Sanders (*below*), some fifty miles west of Cheyenne, the party turned in its equipment and disbanded for the season.

This cairn of skulls and bones, of the buffalo, elk, mountain sheep and deer, impressed Jackson when he saw it near the Fort. It seemed to point a moral. He recalled the "sportsmen" he had known to fire point-blank into the close-packed herd when it came within range of the railroad cars. The useful animals were killed for no other purpose than to make prey for the wolves and the coyotes.

But Jackson was more interested in the future which Hayden's hearty approval of his work was opening up to him. Hayden insisted that Jackson meet him in Washington as soon as possible for confirmation of his appointment as official photographer on the Surveys to come, and a leisurely discussion of the plans for 1871.

WHAT WAS IN COLTER'S HELL

IS appointment to the staff of the Hayden Survey, considered as a link with the larger national life and as a post in which artistic ambition and daily bread might be equated, filled Jackson with enthusiasm. The personal problems and vexations incidental to the sale of his Omaha gallery and the shift of his home to Washington were almost overlooked in the hopeful mood in which he began the year 1871. His new assignment would be a way to win, not wealth, but that better thing, professional recognition.

Meanwhile, Hayden had announced his intention to survey the headwaters of the Yellowstone on his 1871 expedition. Colter's Hell was literally in the papers again.

For all that roaring mining camps and prosperous ranches were flourishing within a hundred miles of the place, until early September, 1869, the Yellowstone's headwaters were still the matter of an elaborate myth. David Folsom, a Montana rancher, had undertaken a private excursion to Yellowstone Lake in 1869, but on his return he valued his reputation as a truthful man too highly to reveal what he had seen to more than a few trusted friends. At their urging, Folsom prepared a literal account of his journey for the *Western Monthly* of Chicago. Only one copy of the July, 1870, issue, in which his story should have appeared, survived a fire at the offices of the magazine.

Folsom's verbal account, however, had stirred the imaginations of a group of Montana men of substance, and they flattered themselves that a confirmation of his findings by them would convince the nation. This group included, among others, Nathaniel Langford, General Henry Washburn, Cornelius Hedges and Lt. Gustavus Doane of the garrison at Fort Ellis, when it set forth in late August, 1870, for an unofficial, civilian survey. Of the careful records kept by the members of the party, Lt. Doane's report slumbered in the War Department's files until 1873; Langford's diary was the basis for articles announcing the wonders of the Yellowstone which appeared in *Scribner's Magazine* during May and June, 1871. With a bland confidence that is somehow comic today, Langford, collector of internal revenue for Montana Territory and a man used to deference in his own bailiwick, was modestly ready for the fame that his articles were sure to bring him.

But not even the authority of *Scribner's* could shield Langford and his friends from the cold blast of unbelief that blew in with every mail. "This Langford is the champion liar of the Northwest," wrote one constant reader to the venerable Josiah Holland, editor of *Scribner's,* and many other letters rang the changes on the Munchausen theme.

Early in 1871, Hayden had heard Langford lecture at Washington, D. C. He was convinced that Langford was telling the truth, for as a member of Raynolds' expedition in 1859, Hayden had seen enough of the country south of the disputed region to know that the Langford claims were more than plausible. And because he had in Jackson and Jackson's camera a means of resolving all popular scepticism concerning mud volcanoes and spouting geysers, he made up his mind on the instant to lead his Survey up the Yellowstone. A photographic record of a place so much in the public mind would be a contribution to science. It would be also an ideal way to dramatize his own work and win support for it from men who might not know silicon from copper but who could appreciate a good show.

It was a young, gay and enthusiastic group which assembled at Ogden, Utah, in the first week of June, 1871; just the kind of a party in which Hayden could inspire the finest loyalty and most devoted sense of duty. Horses, mules, tents and wagons were on the way from Cheyenne by rail. Potato John, who had won his nickname in 1870 by a vain attempt to boil spuds on the high Uinta peaks, was again the chief cook, and many of the packers and teamsters had returned.

Thomas Moran, official artist on the 1871 Survey, was another addition to the party, and one very welcome to Jackson. Fresh from European success as a painter, he was fated to find in his first acquaintance with the American West subjects and natural tints worthy of the grand style, romantic imagination and rich coloring of his master, J. M. W. Turner. In after years, Jackson was fond of referring people who praised his photographs to Moran's magnificent paintings of the same subjects. Meanwhile, he busied himself with his cameras: the 6½ x 8½ he had used on the 1870 expedition and a new 8 x 10 box. They were no longer bundled up, makeshift fashion, in parfleches; each camera was now housed in a specially built case of sole leather, and rubber bags had taken the place of "Hypo's" little keg. He was well pleased with his outfit.

All hands were glad when the expedition left the shadeless, beach camp at Ogden, Utah, on the 10th of June.

Hayden maintained a tenuous link with his professor's chair at Pennsylvania by riding his horse "Patsy" in a frayed but eminently respectable dress coat.

Three days' travel through fat and placid Mormon settlements, carefully tended orchards, and bright gardens brought the expedition to Cache Valley (*above*), whose terraced sides gave evidence of prehistoric Lake Bonneville and its vanished waters.

Once over the divide, they followed the Portneuf River as it flowed in innumerable, small cascades along its irregular lava bed to its junction with the Snake. The Snake was crossed by Taylor's Bridge, and then the party headed north over the wastes of Idaho. Near Hole-In-The-Wall Stage Station, they could see the Teton Range far to the eastward, and Jackson told himself that one day he would know those peaks.

In this sparse country of Idaho, the only Indians encountered were Bannacks, the disgruntled lesser brothers of the Shoshones, who were not at this time hostile. At the *left* is a typical Bannack family occupying a brush tepee.

The family of Bannacks shown *below* were comparative plutocrats in possessing a canvas cover for their shelter.

This was Virginia City, Montana Territory (first named "Varina" after Mrs. Jefferson Davis), when the Hayden Survey party saw it early in July, 1871. The glory had departed from it. The picturesque confusion of miners, dance-hall girls, bad men and stage-drivers had followed the gleam of new gold strikes to Colorado.

Eight years before, a party of prospectors had set out from Bannack City on an exploring trip to the upper Yellowstone. Indians had driven them back from that country, so they made camp on the Gallatin River at a point southwest of the present city of Bozeman. A man named Fairweather chipped a likely-looking rim of rock near camp, and by the end of the day he had panned out one hundred and fifty dollars in gold. The party named the place Alder Gulch, vowed complete secrecy and returned to Bannack City for supplies. But there was no keeping a gold strike secret. In a matter of hours, the rush was on. During the three palmy years that followed the first strike, more than thirty million dollars had been taken out of the Virginia City diggings.

The mushroom town became a legend of wealth and uproar. Hollywood's classic plot of the crooked sheriff in league with the bad men originated in real life at Virginia City.

Henry Plummer, personable, suave, exquisitely dressed and thoroughly evil, had fled there from the clutches of California and Nevada Vigilantes. After frightening the timid incumbent out of town, he was elected Sheriff of Virginia City and Bannack City by popular acclaim. He then chose for deputies about a hundred scoundrels, hand-picked in his ripe experience of men, for the stage-robbing activities he had in mind.

With great executive skill, and even greater assurance (for the good people of the town did not suspect his part until the end), he directed profitable operations in larceny and murder through most of 1863.

Toward the end of that year, the responsible citizens of Montana Territory organized a Vigilance Committee and began to clean things up. Masked men tracked down the "Innocents," as the members of Plummer's gang were used to call one another, and by twos and threes they were given short shrift on the nearest tree. Headstones in the local graveyard still gave evidence of this work when Jackson and the Survey party arrived in Virginia City. "Club-foot George Lane—Hanged," and then the date.

Plummer was among the last to be suspected, but he got his length of rope on January 10, 1864, along with Ned Ray and Buck Stinson. About that time, an old acquaintance, Joseph Alfred Slade (see page 10), was arrested for threatening a magistrate and hanged from the top beam of the town corral's gate. They pulled a dry-goods box from under his feet and he died very penitent, lamenting the absence of the wife he loved so well.

But by 1871, the easily mined surface gold had all been taken, and only a few hopeful souls continued to pan in Alder Gulch. As seen *above*, hydraulic mining methods were being employed with considerable success.

In the picture *below*, the gravel is moving down the flume after the jet has loosened it from the hillside.

Before the Survey group left Virginia City, Jackson went north to photograph Helena, Montana (a polite improvement on the earlier "Crab Town"), where in the fall of 1864 John Cowan had struck it rich at Last Chance Gulch. As seen *above*, it was a thriving place.

Four weeks after leaving Ogden, Utah, Hayden and his party arrived at the last outpost before the mysterious goal of their journey. This was Fort Ellis, on the East Gallatin River, and after it there was a rough trail southward to Colter's Hell.

Near Fort Ellis, in Bridger Canyon, was the rock formation called "The Needle," pictured *right*.

1871

Thomas Moran was rapidly distinguishing himself as woodsman, fisherman and cook. Jackson photographed his artist-friend on horseback and preserved proof of his skill with a trout line.

On the trail southward from Fort Ellis, there was always a hearty welcome in comfortable, if crude-looking, ranch houses.

This building was on Major Pease's ranch, near the Yellowstone River.

At Boteler's ranch (*above*), thirty miles from Fort Ellis on the western bank of the Yellowstone, the Survey expedition transferred its gear from the wagons to pack mules, and began to follow the Washburn-Langford route southward to the volcanic, canyon country. From Hayden down to phlegmatic Potato John, all were eager to see what the wonderland would reveal; around the camp fires, time was spent in talk which might better have been given to sleep.

By day they pushed along a narrow trail, close to the tree-fringed river and over-hung by towering mountains that seemed much closer than they really were. Marks of dragging lodge-poles on the earth testified to Indian parties close at hand, but the Crow camp shown *below* was passed without incident.

The Hayden Survey expedition is seen *above* in full strength as it neared the Montana boundary. The small, wheeled object in the center foreground is an odometer, used to measure the trails. The man riding at the head of the column is Lt. Doane, who had come from Fort Ellis to give Hayden the benefit of his familiarity with the landmarks along the trail.

This was fortunate, for the way ran through deep canyons and over brush-laden spurs of the mountains. Indian trails crossed and re-crossed. Some were clear and fresh; others had long been abandoned. Smoke signals rose from the mountain-sides as the Indians gave notice to one another of alien presences in the valley. Doane said there was little to fear, for the tribes avoided the haunted country of the geysers, and the wretched Sheepeaters who lived there would run from white men.

At the middle canyon, where the trail narrowed almost to extinction and ran high over a spur, the river changed its character. In the words of Doane's report:

"At one point it dashes here and there, lashed to a white foam upon its rocky bed; at another it subsides into a crystal mirror wherever a deep basin occurs in the channel. Numerous small cascades are seen tumbling from the rocky walls at different points, and the river appears from the lofty summits a mere ribbon of foam in the immeasurable distance below. This huge abyss, through walls of flinty lava, has not been worn away by the waters; it is a cleft in the strata brought about by volcanic action, plainly shown by that irregular structure which gives such a ragged appearance to all such igneous formations. Standing on the brink of the chasm, the heavy roaring of the imprisoned river comes to the ear only in a sort of hollow, hungry growl, strongly suggestive of demons in torment below. Lofty pines on the bank of the stream dwindle to shrubs in the dizziness of distance. Everything beneath has a weird, deceptive appearance. The water does not look like water, but like oil. Numerous fish-hawks are seen busily plying their vocation, sailing high above the waters, yet a thousand feet below the spectator. In the clefts of the rocks, hundreds of feet down, bald eagles have their eyries from which we can see them swooping still further into the depths to rob the ospreys of their hard-earned trout. It is grand, gloomy and terrible; a solitude peopled with fantastic ideas; an empire of shadows and turmoil. The great plateau had been recently burned off to drive away the game, and the woods were still on fire in every direction."

Hayden's party left the Washburn-Langford route at Cinnabar Mountain and headed for the Gardiner River. Hayden, himself, described their first discoveries in his report to the Department of the Interior. After passing the junction of the Yellowstone and Gardiner Rivers, the valley up which the Survey moved had walls of volcanic rock, "like the refuse about an old furnace," as Hayden put it.

"The tops of the rounded hills are covered with fragments of basalt and conglomerate, and the variety of sombre colors adds much to the appearance of desolation. One or two depressions, which appear much like volcanic vents, are now filled with water to the brim, forming stagnant lakes fifty to one hundred yards in diameter. We pass over this barren, elevated region for two miles when we descend abruptly to the low bottom which is covered with a thick crust, indicating the former presence of hot springs. At one point a huge stream of hot water, six feet wide and two feet deep flows from beneath the crust.

"Our path led up the hill by the side of a wall of rocks, and we soon came to the most abundant remains of old springs, which, in past times, must have been very active. The steep hill, for nearly a mile, is covered with a thick crust, much decomposed and covered with a moderately thick growth of pines and cedars.

"After ascending the side of the mountain, about a mile above the channel of Gardiner River, we suddenly came in full view of one of the finest displays of nature's architectural skill the world can produce. Before us was a hill two hundred feet high, composed of the deposit of the springs, with a system of step-like terraces which would defy any description by words."

On the next page is Jackson's picture of what they saw; the first picture ever taken in Yellowstone. Thomas Moran is seen examining the forms and colors of the Mammoth Hot Springs.

"The steep sides of the hill were ornamented with a series of semi-circular basins, with margins varying in height and so beautifully scalloped and adorned with a sort of bead-work that the beholder stands amazed. Add to this a snow-white ground, with every variety of shade of scarlet, green and yellow as brilliant as the brightest dyes."

"The pools or basins are of all sizes, from a few inches to six or eight feet in diameter, and from two inches to two feet deep. Even the beautiful series of photographs taken by Mr. Jackson falls far short in fidelity to nature. The photographs fail to give the exquisitely delicate contrasts of coloring."

"At the top of the hill there is a broad, flat terrace (Jupiter Terrace, *above*).
Here we find the largest and most active spring of the group at the present time."

"As we pass up to the base of the principal terrace, we find a large area covered with shallow pools, some of them containing water with all the ornamentations perfect, others fast going to decay and the resulting decomposed sediment as white as snow. Upon this kind of sub-terrace is a remarkable cone, about forty feet in height and twenty feet in diameter at the base. It is undoubtedly the remains of an extinct geyser. We gave it the name of the 'Liberty Cap'."

To quote Hayden again: "Near the mouth of Tower Creek, we can see in the walls of the Canyon the several rows of columns of basalt arrayed in a vertical position, and as regular as if carried and placed in the sides of the gorge by the hand of art."

On the way up the Yellowstone toward Tower Creek, the naturalists of the Survey had used a camp interval to prepare their specimens of bird life for transportation.

The man seated in the right foreground *above* is the mighty master of the skillet, Potato John, whose work was praised by all.

"Our road diverged to the westward of the Yellowstone River," wrote Hayden, "and crossed the northern side of the rim of the basin about a mile west of Mount Washburn. . . . We were able to ride our horses to the very summit."

The picture *above* was taken atop Mount Washburn.

"The view from the summit is one of the finest I have ever seen, and although the atmosphere was somewhat obscured by smoke, yet an area of fifty to a hundred miles radius in every direction could be seen more or less distinctly. We had a first glimpse of the great basin of the Yellowstone, with the Lake, which reminded one much from its bays, indentations and surrounding mountains of the Great Salt Lake. To the south are the Tetons, monarchs of all they survey, their summits covered with perpetual snow. Southwest, an immense area of dense, pine forests extends for one hundred miles. To the north we get a full view of the valley of the Yellowstone, with the lofty ranges that wall it in."

To the *left* the topographers are shown at work.

"Our trail," continued Hayden, "passed over the rim of the basin on the south side of Mount Washburn, and the lowest point was 8774 feet. After passing the divide, we descended the almost vertical sides of the rim into the valley of Cascade Creek at the level of 7787 feet, or about 1000 feet below the divide. Our trail was a tortuous one, to avoid the fallen timber and the dense groves of pine. The country immediately around the creek looked like a beautiful meadow at this date, covered with grass and flowers.

"Cascade Creek flows from the west into the Yellowstone, between the upper and the lower falls. Just before it enters the Yellowstone, it flows over a series of ridges, making one of the most beautiful cascades in the region. As this little cascade is seen from the east branch of the Yellowstone, dividing up into a number of little streams and rushing down from ledge to ledge until it reaches the bed of the river, it presents a picture of real beauty.

"But the objects of deepest interest in this region are the Grand Canyon and the Falls. It is only through the eye that the mind can gather anything like an adequate conception of them. As we approached the margin of the canyon, we could hear the suppressed roar of the falls, resembling distant thunder.

"Standing near the margin and looking down the canyon, an immense chasm or cleft in the basalt, with its sides 1200 to 1500 feet high, and decorated with the most brilliant colors, the rocks weathered into an almost unlimited variety of forms and here and there a pine sending its roots into the clefts on the sides as if struggling with uncertainty for existence, the mind of the onlooker is seized with impressions of grandeur. Mr. Moran exclaimed with a kind of regretful enthusiasm that these tints were beyond the resources of human art. The waters of the Yellowstone seem, as it were to gather themselves into one compact mass and plunge over the descent of 350 feet in foam as white as snow. Upon the yellow, nearly vertical western side, the mist mostly falls, and for 300 feet from the bottom the wall is covered with a thick matting of mosses, sedges, grasses and other vegetation of the most vivid green, which have sent their small roots into the softened rocks and are nourished by the ever-ascending spray."

On the next page is shown one of the pictures Jackson made in an attempt to realize by photography what Moran's brush and Hayden's pen despaired of . . . the perfection of natural form in the Lower Falls of the Yellowstone.

The Yellowstone River ran tranquilly through a broad valley beyond the Falls, and the Survey party reached the Lake without too much difficulty. But the journey around the Lake had to be made through heavy forests, swampy ground, fallen timber thickly intertwined, and at the shore line a rubble of volcanic debris.

Immense numbers of pelicans and swans sailed in fleets along the Lake. The low, flat islands were white with birds at the close of day. In the woods were mockingbirds and grouse, and guide-birds, resembling blackbirds but larger, which hopped and flew ahead of the party, waiting while the men rested, and then leading on again as soon as they prepared to march.

It was clear that the whole basin had been virtually abandoned by the Indians. Only a few shelters of logs were found, rotted and tumbling down, and a few poles still upright in remains of former summer camps. There were no fresh trails anywhere.

The camp shown *below* was pitched on the southwest arm of Yellowstone Lake.

Despite Lt. Doane's familiarity with the region, the journey northwestward was none too easy. It was all through broken country, over rocky ridges and swampy terraces, until they reached a gorge of lava, two hundred feet deep, wherein a torrent ran roaring. This was the Fire Hole River, and the route now ran northward along the river's course.

The canyon slowly descended to a level with the stream; at one point, the water tumbled gaily over rocks in a miniature but lovely cascade.

Scattered along both banks of the river were boiling springs and craters. These varied from two to twelve feet across.

Jim Bridger, John Colter, the outraged Nathaniel Langford, all the eloquent company of scouts, prospectors and trappers who had retailed stories of this fabulous place, were now handsomely vindicated. From camp on the bank of the Fire Hole River, the men of the Hayden Survey looked up the rolling, irregularly-shaped valley at the grandest display of geysers in the world. On either side the mountain ridges rose fifteen hundred feet; the steep, dark lava walls were heavily wooded.

"Soon after reaching camp," said Hayden, "a tremendous rumbling was heard, shaking the ground in every direction, and soon a column of steam burst forth from a crater near the edge of the east side of the river. Following the steam, arose, by a series of impulses, a column of water apparently six feet in diameter to the height of two hundred feet, while the steam ascended a thousand feet or more. After the display is over, the water settles down in the basin several inches and the temperature slowly falls to 150 degrees. Nothing could exceed the crystal clearness of the water. This we called the Grand Geyser.

"The Castle Geyser receives its name from its resemblance to the ruins of an old castle as one enters the valley from the east. The entire mound is about forty feet high, and the chimney twenty feet. This has undoubtedly been one of the most active and powerful geysers in the basin; it still keeps up a great roaring inside, and every few moments throws out a column of water to the height of ten or fifteen feet; all around it are most beautifully ornamented reservoirs that receive the surplus waters."

Crater of the Grand Geyser.

A distant view of the Castle Geyser in action.

"The Giant Geyser has a crater like a broken horn," wrote Hayden, "and while my party were in the basin played at one time one hour and twenty minutes, throwing the water up to a height of 140 feet."

The crater of the Giant is shown *left*.

"Our search for new wonders leading us across the Fire Hole River, we ascended a gentle, incrusted slope, and came suddenly upon a large, oval aperture with scalloped edges, the diameters of which were 18 and 25 feet, the sides corrugated and covered with a grayish-white deposit which was distinctly visible at the depth of 100 feet below the surface. No water could be discovered, but we could hear it gurgling and boiling at a great distance below. Suddenly it began to rise and send out huge masses of steam, causing a general stampede of our party. When within forty feet of the surface, it became stationary and we returned to look down at it. It was foaming and surging at a terrible rate, occasionally emitting small jets of hot water nearly to the mouth of the orifice.

"All at once it seemed seized with a fearful spasm and rose with incredible rapidity, hardly affording us time to flee to a safe distance. It burst from the orifice with terrific momentum, rising in a column the full size of the immense aperture to the height of sixty feet, and through and out of the apex of this vast, aqueous mass five or six lesser jets were projected to the marvellous height of 250 feet.

"This grand eruption continued for twenty minutes. We were standing on the side of the geyser nearest the sun, whose gleams filled the sparkling column of water and spray with myriad rainbows, dipping and fluttering hither and thither, disappearing only to be succeeded by others. The minute globules into which the spent jets were diffused when falling sparkled like a shower of diamonds. Around every shadow which the denser clouds of vapor, interrupting the sun's rays, cast upon the column, could be seen a luminous circle radiant with all the colors of the prism and resembling the halo of glory represented in paintings as surrounding the head of Divinity. All that we had seen seemed tame in comparison with the grandeur and beauty of this display. This geyser we named the Giantess."

The Giantess is seen *above* in a quieter mood than that just described.

"A hundred yards distant from the Giantess was a siliceous cone, very symmetrical but slightly corrugated on its exterior surface, 3 feet in height and 5 feet in diameter at the base. Among so many wonders it had almost escaped notice. While we were at breakfast, a column of water entirely filling the crater shot from it, which, by accurate triangular measurement we found to be 219 feet in height. We named it the Beehive."

The Fountain Geyser, whose crater is shown *above,* lay northward of those previously described by Hayden.

Mud springs were numerous along the Fire Hole River.

"On our return to the Lake from this basin," said Hayden, "we passed up the Fire Hole River to its source in the divide.

"Early in the morning, as we were leaving the valley, the grand old geyser which stands sentinel at the head of the valley gave us a magnificent parting display, and with little or no preliminary warning it shot up a column of water to the height of 100 to 150 feet. By a succession of impulses, it seemed to hold the column steadily for the space of fifteen minutes, the great mass of water falling directly back into the basin and flowing over the edges and down the sides in large streams. When the action ceases, the water recedes beyond sight and nothing is heard but the occasional escape of steam until another exhibition occurs.

"This is one of the most accommodating geysers in the basin, and during our stay played once an hour quite regularly. On account of its regularity and its position overlooking the valley, Messrs. Langford and Doane called it 'Old Faithful'. It has built up a crater about 20 feet high around its base, and all about it are decorations similar to those previously described."

Jackson's photograph of the crater of Old Faithful is seen *below,* and on the preceding page is the same "accommodating" geyser in action.

BEFORE CONGRESS

O N March 1, 1872, President Ulysses S. Grant set his name to one bill which not even Horace Greeley and the rampant Liberal Republicans, who scented a scandal in the Executive's every act, could censure or decry. By the terms of this bill, the wealth of canyons, geysers, lakes and mountains around the headwaters of the Yellowstone was reserved forever to the people of the United States and established as the first of our National Parks. Hayden added a brief comment on this action of Congress to his printed report:

"On the 18th of December, 1871," he wrote, "a bill was introduced into the Senate of the United States by the Honorable S. C. Pomeroy to set apart a certain tract of land lying near the headwaters of the Yellowstone River as a public park. About the same time a similar bill was offered in the House of Representatives by Honorable William H. Clagett, Delegate from Montana. After due consideration in the Committees on Public Lands in both Houses, the bill was reported favorably. In the Senate it was advocated ably by Messrs. Pomeroy, Edmunds, Trumbull, Anthony and others. In the House, the remarks of Honorable H. L. Dawes were so clear and forcible that the bill passed at once without opposition."

And after a few generalities, he continued:

"That our legislators, at a time when the public opinion is so strong against appropriating the public domain for any purpose however laudable, should reserve for the benefit and instruction of the people a tract of 3,578 square miles, is an act that should cause universal joy throughout the land. This noble deed may be regarded as a tribute from our legislators to science."

The demure language, quoted above, makes it all sound so easy. The National Park concept would appear to have been born painlessly and to slow, solemn music. But as always, behind the polite jargon of a government report hides a story of effort and strain and adroit diplomacy. It had better be told from the beginning.

Sprawled about the camp-fire on the night of September 19, 1870, a full year before Hayden had come to the Yellowstone, the men of the Washburn-Langford expedition had fallen into the talkative mood which comes with physical weariness and mental excitement. Camp had been pitched at the junction of the Fire Hole and Gibbon Rivers, and they were homeward bound for Virginia City after witnessing Nature's ways in her laboratory as she worked at the building of earth. They had seen wonders which had no match in the known world.

The imaginations of some of the men had run immediately to schemes for personal gain: quarter-sections to be claimed near the canyon; hotels to be built overlooking the choicest geysers; a golden horde of tourists to be guided at so much a head! It was a grand and gaudy prospect. But Cornelius Hedges, judge and potent member of the Montana bar, had struck in with a violent "no." There should be no such fate for a place so rarely beautiful, he said. Only a great national preserve, removed forever by law from commercial exploitation, could save the Yellowstone for all the people.

Under the September stars, his eloquence was powerful. There was some grumbling dissent of course, but Nathaniel Langford lay awake half the night, turning over and over in his mind his friend's novel inspiration. All the next day, as they rode through dark, narrow canyons and over heavily wooded ridges toward Montana, the party wrangled and disputed, but long before they reached Virginia City it was clear that Langford, Washburn and Hedges would do all in their considerable power to block any land-rush into the Yellowstone headwaters. The majority of the group agreed with the leaders.

The next effective steps were taken during the following summer at Helena, Montana. It appeared that David Folsom had discussed the possibility of reserving the Yellowstone for park purposes in a talk with General Washburn, before the 1870 expedition had left to explore the region. And so, encouraged by this and other local sentiment, Hedges and Langford called during August, 1871, on the newly-elected Delegate to Congress from Montana Territory, the Honorable William H. Clagett. They had drafted a plan, and Clagett gave it his enthusiastic support. All of them realized that they must act in haste before too many enterprising exploiters could make claims and so-called "improvements" in the proposed park area.

While the Helena conference was on, the Hayden Survey was making its way up the Fire Hole Valley toward Boteler's Ranch and the end of its mission for that year. Early in the fall of 1871, Hayden arrived in Washington, and Jackson reported a few weeks later at the offices of the Survey on Pennsylvania Avenue, and went quietly to work making extra prints of his most recent photographs. Hayden had found that Jackson's magnificent pictures could be appreciated only from actual photographic prints. He could afford to take no chances with inferior reproductions.

Langford had come to Washington, meanwhile, to advise Delegate Clagett in the final stages of the National Park project. As they worked on the bill to be presented in Congress, they ran into trouble over the precise boundaries of the area, and, at Clagett's suggestion, Langford called on Hayden for an exact description of the place.

Now, despite the trivial disputes over proper credit for founding the Yellowstone National Park, from this point on to the passage of the bill in the House on January 30, and in the Senate on February 27, 1872, there is a very noticeable "Hayden touch" in the way things were handled. Hayden supplied the true boundaries of the park and a map. Beyond this, it is fair to credit the quick-witted Hayden, skilled in coaxing his yearly subsidy out of the Congressmen of the Gilded Age, rather than a freshman Delegate from a Territory or a relatively obscure civil servant, with "the most intensive canvass accorded any bill."

Each member of the House was visited personally by Langford, Hayden or Clagett; the Senators received the same flattering attention; the Secretary of the Interior was induced to give the bill his public approval. Specimens of the mineral wealth and the animal life of the region were displayed and explained. The trump card was held for the last.

At just the right moment, prints of the Jackson photographs were placed on the desks of all Senators and members of the House. Handsomely bound folio volumes of the photographs, neatly captioned, and bearing the name of the recipient in gold, were distributed among those perennial, shadowy gentlemen who were believed to have an "influence" beyond their immediate official position. It was these actual pictures of the wonders of the upper Yellowstone that clinched the vote in favor of the first National Park.

On the following pages are shown nine of the pictures the Congressmen saw, as they prepared to cast their votes that cold January day in 1872.

Mammoth Hot Springs (see Hayden's account on pages 121 to 125).

Summit of Jupiter Terrace, looking north (see Hayden's account on page 125).

Tower Falls.

The Grand Canyon of the Yellowstone (see Hayden's account on page 129).

Grand Canyon of the Yellowstone from the foot of the Lower Falls.

Great Falls of the Yellowstone (see Hayden's account on page 129).

View of the Upper Geyser Basin from "Old Faithful" (see Hayden's account on page 142).

The Crater of the Grotto Geyser.

The Crater of the Castle Geyser (see Hayden's account on page 133).

TO THE HIGH PLACES

JACKSON set the field-glasses down carefully on one of the camera cases. From where he stood in Pierre's Hole, he was close enough to the Grand Teton to make out the structure of its gaunt peak, but there would be clambering and trouble enough before he could get a view of it that would satisfy him. He had not come this far to do a second-rate job.

The old fur traders had given names to these "holes" in the Rockies, these mountain valleys snug beneath sentinel peaks and watered by icy streams that ran in broad ribbons of surrounding green toward the passes to the plains. Wild flowers shone everywhere. Here, where summer was a fleeting season, there was a curious mingling of spring and fall blooms, of violet and strawberry, geraniums, monkshood and gentians. Clematis twined along the banks of the innumerable, small, swampy creeks. Game sheltered in these valleys from the waste plains below, and from the wild winds above timberline. The Indians knew them of old as homes; as early as 1826 the Mountain Men had chosen them for camp-sites and places of rendezvous.

The eastern wall of the Teton Range looked down into the mirror of Jackson's Lake.

From the north shore of this Lake to the mouth of the Little Grosventre River was Jackson's Hole, and through it flowed the early reaches of the Snake as it began its long sweep to the Columbia.

Pierre's River coursed down from the western rampart of the Tetons into Henry Fork of the Snake River. Its broad valley, twenty-five miles long, was called Pierre's Hole, after a fabled chieftain who had discovered the river and the valley, and it was famous in western lore for a bloody, all-day siege of raiding Grosventres who had run into the Trappers' Rendezvous of 1832 just as it was breaking up for the season.

To this new country Jackson had come in the middle of July, 1872. He had followed the rampaging Snake to Henry Fork, shifted his equipment from wagons to mule back at the mouth of the Pierre, and then followed the vagaries of that stream as far as the present camp within sight of his towering objectives.

By this time he had become something of an authority on mules. A mule looked stubborn and was stubborn, but on the steep mountain trails her surefootedness made her invaluable. *Below* is seen Stage One in the morning ritual of packing. Old Molly is asking her mulish soul just what she can do to drive the packers wild. She was never at a loss for ideas of this kind.

In Stage Two, *above,* the despondent droop of Molly's head is caused by her recognition of an expert touch as the packers tighten the cinch with boot and hand. She will not be able to pull her usual tenderfoot trick of bellying-out with a deep breath, so that the cinch will slip when she lets her breath go.

The pack mule *above,* at the *right,* after a month of toting the heavier equipment, deliberately took a long header into the Gallatin River as a gesture of protest.

The pensive, delicate artist-type shown *right* was named "Dolly" and never stooped to vulgar pack-loads.

Mule troubles notwithstanding, Jackson rejoiced in this season of 1872. His photographic division, now five men strong, had been declared an independent unit of the Hayden Survey, and the decision to accompany James Stevenson's party to the heart of the high places had been Jackson's own decision. This freedom of action meant much more to him than the fine, praiseful talk of the notables in Washington. The various Survey parties in the field were to meet Hayden at the Yellowstone headwaters in mid-August, but Jackson had three precious weeks to pierce the mysteries of the Teton Range and stand on the roof of the mountains.

Wild strawberries grew abundantly in the neighborhood of the base camp shown *above*, and the streams nearby were choked with beaver dams; but Coulter, the botanist, could find no trace of "the tangle of vines from tree to tree," which Washington Irving had declared characteristic of Pierre's Hole.

As the other men looked curiously through the glasses at the far-off peaks, Jackson sat down to puzzle out the problems of equipment and terrain he would have to solve before he had a close-up view of the Grand Teton under his lens. Melted snow would make an adequate water supply for plate-washing, but would the cameras and other apparatus survive the rough journey?

For eight days Jackson and his associates climbed wearily over piles of loose debris and over steep rock-slopes, over masses of snow above timberline where mountain flowers at times pushed fragile blossoms above the white, and where hundreds of numbed grass-hoppers lay in little snow-beds which the heat of their bodies had thawed. But the dizzy gorge of Glacier Creek cut across the approach to the Grand Teton, as may be seen in the long-range view *below*.

During the search for the perfect point of view, the photographic division bivouacked in camps like the one shown *above*. The game was plentiful in this isolated region; big-horned mountain sheep, bears and elk ranged over the high plateau, and one of the men got a young moose, which may be seen *above* in quarters.

On the ninth day out from the main camp, Jackson and his men followed a shallow valley up to a gap in the rock wall. To the left of this gap an immense snow-drift sloped down more than a hundred feet; to the right rose an almost vertical cliff. A trail was tramped out in the snow and the group picked its way along the snowy ledge and through the gap. Then, bearing a little to the right, they found themselves on the very crest of the western wall of the gorge. The Grand Teton, 13,747 feet in height, rose directly in front as seen on the facing page.

A few feet back from the edge of the abyss, Jackson knelt beside his little tent "dark-box" and prepared his wet-plates.

On the lonely rim of the canyon, Jackson knew the exalted feeling that comes with a perfected ambition. He had labored to find the best angle for his portrait of the giant, and he was satisfied that he had found it. But as he packed away his equipment and prepared to retrace his steps, he knew that this was only the beginning. The high places were in his blood. They were no longer places imagined from the foothills.

But he worried about the change that seemed to be taking place in his character, the stirring in him of the mountaineer's contempt for the advantages of society. Just as Jim Bridger had said once, city streets were canyons, but cold and forbidding ones where the sun shone weakly and men grew restless. Would there be a fundamental clash between these convictions and an idea he was slowly maturing relative to Miss Emilie Painter, of Blair, Nebraska? He couldn't be sure.

Over snow-slides and by rugged, trailless country, Jackson and his men made their way back to the base camp in Teton Canyon, or Pierre's Hole, and found that the hunters had been putting their time to good use. In the picture *below,* Joe Clark and Jose are bringing in a load of elk meat.

It was time Stevenson's party, and Jackson's, should start northward if they expected
to meet Hayden at the appointed time. The whole company left camp on August 2. A
rough journey it was, up Henry Fork through dense growths of young pine and over the
spiny ridges between the tributary streams, until they entered the open, grassy basin about
Henry's Lake. At the head of the Lake was Sawtelle's Ranch (*above*) where they were
entertained by the owner and his partner, Wurtz. A mowing machine was in operation
near the ranch, and a mass of hay was spread out to cure in the hot sun. Sawtelle told
the Survey men that he and Wurtz had tried to raise stock, but the horseflies and gnats
that bred in the swampy lake had driven them into the fish business. They hauled fish
fifty miles to Virginia City, but the profit made the haul worth while.

Jackson noted in his diary that the meeting of all the units of the Hayden Survey on August 16 in the Lower Fire Hole Basin was as jovial an assembly as one of the old Trappers' Rendezvous. The picture *above* does not appear to bear out this statement. Serious eating, rather than wassail, would appear to be the work in hand.

On the way home, as the party followed the Gallatin River northward, the road ran over rock slides and stumbling rubble for more than ten miles. At the point shown *right* the misguided mule made her expensive gesture of protest (see page 161).

Arched Falls (*left*) was at the base of
Mount Blackmore. The party had reached
Montana now, and were within a few miles
of Fort Ellis.

In this same general vicinity, Jackson photographed one of the small, park-like
stretches along the Gallatin, and caught a fine view of Palace Butte, as shown *below.*

In the study *above*, made at the base camp, the two men directly in front of the tent are not old scouts, but the eminent geologists, Doctors Peals and Turnbull.

So ended the campaign of 1872. Hayden had told his men nothing of his plans for the following year, but Jackson hoped that the Survey would point again to the high places.

HIGH PLACES SOUTHWARD

"NOT a white man was killed in the Department of the Platte during 1872," said the Commissioner of Indian Affairs in his report for that year. This happy condition was not to obtain during 1873. Despite the tour of opulent Eastern cities arranged to convince Red Cloud and his head men that civilization and agriculture paid off handsomely, the Sioux tribesmen were neither sold on reservation life nor resigned to it. About four hundred and fifty lodges under Sitting Bull and other chiefs were reported hostile, and these kept carefully away from the gewgaw-baited traps at the Agencies. Good Agency Sioux, observing the free life of their brothers in Wyoming and Montana, were beginning to regret the trade-goods and fancy-dress that had put them in the condition of the Town Mouse in the fable.

Trouble was in the air. The anxious tone of the Indian Agents' reports to Washington caused Hayden to transfer Survey operations for 1873 to the Colorado Rockies. His foresight was fully justified in August, when at Tongue River, Montana, occurred the first of the incidents which climaxed three years later in the Custer massacre on the Little Big Horn. Besides, the railroads were pushing down to Denver and southward, and it was high time the nation had some scientific knowledge of the resources of yet another new domain.

Not fifteen years before, the Russell party of prospectors had found gold some seventy miles from Pike's Peak, and the "Pike's Peak or bust" rush began. Broken merchants, speculators, foreclosed farmers, foreign adventurers, gamblers and much of the human debris in the wake of the 1857 Panic washed down to Denver and disappointment. These "quick-killing" gentry had no interest in the region other than the sudden wealth a lucky scratch on its soil might provide.

As the spring of 1859 turned to summer, there were strikes at Central, forty miles from Denver, and golden rumors from the banks of the South Platte near the new town of Fairplay. As 1860 began its course, the gold seekers were hard at work around the headwaters of the Arkansas River. The mining "towns" looked more like sloppy military encampments, with their log huts, tents and one-story frame buildings huddled cheek by jowl. The saloons did a land-office business, but there were churches, too, and "opera houses" where travelling troupes played current drama. Outside the gambling houses, bands played cheerful tunes to attract the miner and his buckskin bag of precious dust, eighteen dollars to the ounce in the ever-ready pair of brass scales that stood on every counter.

By 1870 the surface gold was gone and ore-reduction methods required to get at the deeper veins were beyond the skill or the means of the single miner. The Eastern promoter and his "wildcat" stock-selling ventures began to dominate the scene. The pocketbooks of the gullible were nobly harvested by alleged "Professors" who had worked out elaborate chemical processes for reducing low-grade ore. Slowly, the responsible people of the Territory turned to agriculture and the less spectacular mining of silver. The boom times were over, and the "Crime of '73" rang down the curtain on quick and easy wealth in Colorado for over twenty years.

William Henry Jackson was ready for the high places southward. He made an early start from Washington and reached the base camp, three miles outside Denver, on May 14, 1873. His instructions gave him plenty of scope, and not a little uneasiness. He was ordered to range at will over the entire territory under survey, and carry in his division young Coulter, now a full-fledged botanist, and Lt. Carpenter, an entomologist on leave from his Army post. Two experienced packers and Potato John, the cook, were also under his direction.

It was all very well, thought he, to sit in an office on Pennsylvania Avenue and jab carelessly at a possibly accurate map and say "here and here and there." But as he looked around him in camp, the mountains were awfully remote and challenging and many. The Teton country had been reasonably restricted in size and the objectives had been obvious, but now the whole Front Range of the Rockies had been handed him as an objective. There were high places and to spare.

Only a few of the Survey men had arrived in camp ahead of Jackson, and one of them took him firmly and kindly under his wing. This was J. T. Gardner, chief topographer, who had been transferred from King's Survey of the Fortieth Parallel when that group wound up its field work at the end of the preceding season. For a man still under thirty, Gardner had had a remarkable career. He had supervised much fortification work for the Ordnance Department during the Civil War, and the calculations of mountain elevations to be published by the King Survey were the results of his activity and skill. He had, above all, the gift of realizing the larger implications in any task he attempted. We have no record of what was actually said that first evening in camp, but we can be sure that as Jackson stared down at the neat marks in India ink on the sketch map and listened to Gardner's clear, confident advice, he gave his usual ready allegiance to a man who knew more than he did. In his own quick imagination, the marks on the crumpled paper became the earth-rooted giants they stood for, each with its legends and the story of its discovery by white men, each with its lonely eminence in the convulsive upthrust of earth's skin men called the Rocky Mountains.

"We'll get off by the 24th of May," Gardner went on, touching the spots on the map lightly with his pencil, "You take a bee-line for Long's Peak and then work down along the Range to Gray's. Watch out for the toll-gate people at Georgetown; they're robbers.

Argentine Pass will be clear. Then work around by Pike's Peak to Manitou, and cut across from there to meet the boss at Fairplay. Get there by the 10th of July."

"What happens after the 10th?" Jackson asked, "I'd like to have supplies ordered in case we head too far away from Denver."

"Hayden thinks we'll work around the head of the Arkansas," Gardner replied. He looked up from the map and sat, tapping his pencil against his teeth. "Ever hear of the Mountain of the Holy Cross?" Jackson had heard of it. "Everybody talks about it and nobody sees it. I'd like to fix that." Gardner smiled. "Hayden doesn't know it yet, but I think we'll pay it a visit."

Midway in the Snowy Range stood Long's Peak (*above*), a king among his peers. Stephen Long had a noble monument for his efforts in 1820, when the second, official exploration of the West had been led by him up to the foot of the great divide.

The photographic division was encamped in the lower end of Estes Park. The picture of the simple life *left* shows, left to right, Coulter, Lt. Carpenter, two unnamed packers, Potato John and Jackson.

Near Bald Mountain, the panorama of the Snowy Range (*above*) opened out across Red Rock Lake.

The going was hard through woods, past deserted mining camps, upward and over fresh snow to a point in Argentine Pass, shown *below*—elevation about eleven thousand feet. The now-familiar photographic tent may be seen in the left foreground.

Jackson led a single, camera-laden mule from the camp in Argentine Pass up to where his lens overlooked the twin peaks *above*. Gray's Peak, to the left, rose a scant ten feet higher than the 14,264 feet of Torrey's Peak, to the right.

On the descent, rather than pay tolls at the gate the citizens of Georgetown had thrown across the main road, the party took to the hills and canyons, where soft soil

under the animals' feet made the path perilous. It was a foolish economy and consumed in delay what it saved in cash.

The photographic division had left the peaks of the Snowy Range behind them by June 28 and were making a quick push for Manitou. Here, most of the party rested; but Jackson took a busman's holiday in the neighborhood of Pike's Peak.

Framed in the gateway to the Garden of the Gods, Pike's Peak (*above*) shadowed the lesser mountains of the Rampart Range and was a symbol of the western high places to the great body of Americans who had never crossed the Mississippi.

The red sandstone rocks of the gateway, shown close at hand *below*, had been fretted by the elements into an irregular beauty.

The "Major Domo" (*right*) in Glen Eyrie near the foot of Pike's Peak was another of these grotesque sculpturings.

And very properly in a Garden of the Gods, there were "Cathedral Spires," shown *below*.

Monument Park, north of the Garden, boasted these heathen idols of wind-eroded rock.

Near Palmer Lake, a natural arch (*right*) jutted out under Citadel Rock.

The Profile Rocks shown *below,* and indeed this whole vicinity, testified to a continuing war of wind and flying sand against the rocky face of the earth.

THE far-scattered groups of the Hayden Survey met with their chief at Fairplay in mid-July. Silver had been struck in 1871 in the Park Range, and this little town of Fairplay on the South Platte had become the focus of a considerable mining district. Early arrivals at the scene of the strike had set up regulations which limited claims along Tarryall Creek to not more than one hundred and fifty feet. Later comers had rebelled against these regulations and founded a new settlement where "fair play" was guaranteed all comers. The town was booming in the usual style of mining towns, but the men of the Survey had work to do and piously averted their eyes.

Hayden and Gardner were to travel together for the rest of the season and Jackson was to follow them across the Sawatch Range to the Elk Mountains. Hayden concluded his orders with the hope they might have time to explore the Mountain of the Holy Cross. Jackson smiled to himself at the success of Gardner's propaganda. And still it would be no mere sight-seeing jaunt. There was genuine public interest in the mysterious mountain.

William Brewer had seen from Gray's Peak, some time in 1869, a mountain peak "forty miles away with a cross of pure white, a mile high, suspended against its side." Long before Brewer, prospectors had reported seeing it across great distances, but a near view seemed peculiarly elusive. The mountain itself, the farthest north peak of the Sawatch Range, was real enough and reasonably well-known, but its characteristic sign had a way of disappearing on close approach.

If such a thing exists, thought Jackson, the Hayden Survey will find it.

On the western rim of the Upper Arkansas basin, Jackson took the panorama of the Sawatch Range shown *above*. Upper Twin Lake is in the foreground. An old pirate named Derry, who claimed to own the land around the Lake, tried without success to collect twenty-five cents a head for grazing privileges over his sagebrush.

As they clambered through thick timber toward the summit of La Plata Peak (about eighteen miles from Leadville), the mules showed signs of mutiny at twelve thousand feet elevation. The men packed chemicals, cameras and plates on their shoulders and

gasped their way up the final two thousand feet. Jackson thought that the view northward over the Sawatch, shown *above,* was worth the effort.

The natural arch shown *left* was discovered during the return to camp when men and animals came tumbling down a slide into the icy waters of the creek it spanned.

Westward by Indian trails the party moved from the La Plata region to Rock Creek at the foot of Snow Mass Mountain. Here, Jackson made a study of his associates against a noble background of the Elk Mountains (*below*).

It was now August 17, and if the Survey were going to find the Mountain of the Holy Cross, all else must be dropped and the trail set eastward and then north through Tennessee Pass to the logical approach by way of Eagle River Canyon.

Gardner proposed to climb the mountain in order to make a primary triangulation from its summit for his detail maps. He was as happy as a boy on the Fourth of July. Even Hayden had shaken off some of the end-of-season weariness that always followed on his vast expense of nervous energy to join in the adventurous spirit of the expedition.

The picture *below* shows the party at dinner in Eagle River Canyon after an uneventful crossing of the easy but heavily wooded Tennessee Pass. From left to right are seated Hayden, Stevenson, W. S. Holman, two unidentified men, Gardner, W. D. Whitney and W. H. Holmes.

Cross Creek, a tributary of Eagle River, threw the difficulties shown *above* in the way of Gardner's best efforts as a guide. Fallen timber, rocks and swamps reduced the pace of the journey to five miles a day.

Hard and persistent axe work cut a trail to a point that overlooked the valley of the Sheep Back Rocks, or Roches Moutonnées, to be seen *above*. By all that was honest in maps, the snow-splashed mountain dead ahead was Holy Cross. From this point, no snowy cross was visible on its bleak flank, but the north-east face looked down into a valley among the high places, and Notch Mountain to the left might be hiding the wonder behind its granite shoulder.

Shortly after dawn on the morning of August 23, while Gardner set off to attempt a direct ascent of the Mountain of the Holy Cross, Jackson and his assistants followed the course of Cross Creek over fallen timber white with frost and through dripping thickets of willow toward Notch Mountain.

Jackson soon outdistanced his companions. Cold mist swirled about him as he worked his way very cautiously up to Notch's naked crest. He felt at once afraid and excited, alone in a sea of cottonny white. And then, through a sudden rift of the clouds, he stared out over the gorge at the Holy Cross. It was true. Deep-packed in crevasses, eternal snow manifested the eternal symbol.

When the others arrived, excitement ran high. But the clouds closed solidly, and a vigil until light failed won no opportunity for a photograph. Hungry and shivering, they returned to a temporary camp near timberline.

Sunday, August 24, dawned bright and clear. The sleepless men hustled the camera up the fifteen hundred feet from camp to the summit, where a warm and brilliant sun had already started rivulets running from the snow banks. The Mountain of the Holy Cross stood revealed for the first time to watchers close at hand.

The first photograph ever taken of the Mountain of the Holy Cross.

THE PEAKS OF SAN JUAN

THE first picture of the Mountain of the Holy Cross won for Jackson the ungrudging applause of his colleagues; the sincerest compliment made him was Thomas Moran's choice of the same subject for what proved to be one of his finest paintings. But the Washington winter of 1873 was, otherwise, a harsh and anxious time. Jay Cooke and Company, the banking house whose missionary, bond-selling zeal had provided the sinews of war for the Union armies, suspended payment in the middle of September and carried down in its fall a host of lesser enterprises, banks, merchants and manufacturers. The Panic of 1873 was on, and there would be hard times until 1878.

Up through the spring of 1874, the sessions of Congress were loud with charges and counter-charges as each party tried to fix responsibility for the disaster on the other. All Washington was much more concerned with personal survival than national recovery, and it was small wonder that the moguls of the Department of the Interior, busily covering up the trail of land speculators to their front office, should have left the financial appropriations for scientific surveys far down on the list of things to do.

At all events, the third week in July, 1874, found Jackson and his division beguiling the idle hours in camp near Clear Creek by organizing flat races for the riding mules. The entries are shown *below*.

The mountains would wait. They had kept their stations a long time. And there was something reassuring about Colorado after a winter in Washington.

When the orders came, and if they did, Jackson was to march far southward, through the familiar glories of Estes Park, and Middle and South Parks, to the rugged San Juan Mountains near the borders of Utah, Arizona and New Mexico. These were high places of a majesty equal to that of the cold peaks in northern and central Colorado, but of a different character. Their massive walls, only lately scarred with prospect-holes and pits, shadowed to the south a warm desert and mesa country, a place of arid ravines, piñon and juniper trees, steady sun in a sky like turquoise, and little water. Indians dwelt there who were a different breed from those of the Plains, a less transient, an older people. Long ago, Coronado had searched for the Seven Golden Cities through the sandy wastes south of the San Juan; in 1849, Lt. J. H. Simpson of the Army brought back a tale of great deserted cities asleep up the remote reaches of Chaco Canyon. The light-fingered Navaho and the fierce Utes roamed over this country, and on occasion bands of Comanches howled up from the South. Whites and Indians spoke the gritty Spanish of Mexico. Time stood still around the central trading town of Santa Fe.

At long last, Jackson and his men were ordered to take the trail. The heavy rains had turned the earth into a thick paste; the brand-new *aparejos* had been badly packed and kept twisting about on the backs of the impatient mules; the inexperienced, new men were hard to break into the ways of the West. The buoyant good humor of Ernest Ingersoll, correspondent of the *New York Tribune* but carried on the muster rolls under the noncommittal title of "naturalist," was a consolation for Jackson in his troubles.

Jackson took this picture from the summit of Berthoud Pass, looking north toward Middle Park. The man with the gun is Harry Yount, game hunter for the Survey and the first ranger of the Yellowstone National Park.

On the journey from Berthoud Pass through the Parks and over the divides to Poncha Pass, through San Luis Valley heavy with summer haze and up the Saguache River, Jackson hurried his men along toward their first, big objective, the Indian Agency at Los Pinos. But he could not resist the view north over Middle Park, from the mouth of the Blue River, shown *above*.

The tepees pictured *below*, surrounded by flocks of domestic animals, belonged to a band of Utes encountered in Cochetopa Pass. Some five miles away, the buildings of the Los Pinos Agency were clearly visible to Jackson and his group.

The Utes were men with a grievance. Since 1850, when the Mormons pushed them out of the Salt Lake Basin, down to 1873 when Chief Ouray (shown *right*) ceded their rich Colorado mountains to the United States in exchange for nothing in particular, the Ute experience of white men in the mass had been bad. A restless, suspicious race of warlike horsemen, they failed to see how gold and silver strikes in the San Juan Mountains altered solemn treaties entered into in good faith. So long as the economic expansion of the United States was symbolized by a lawless horde of white invaders who killed their game and mistreated their people, they were opposed to it.

When Jackson met them at Los Pinos, the young men had decided to warn all whites off land secured to the Utes by treaties before 1873. In their view of things, Ouray had no right to glorify himself by giving away what the Ute nation owned in common.

Ouray, sometimes called the only outstanding personality ever developed by his people, had been eloquent in support of the claims of the United States at the treaty conferences of 1863 and 1868. Like Washakie (see page 92), he realized the futility of individual, tribal warfare against the whites. He does not appear, however, to have been above making almost any concessions to the United States, so long as his own comfort and authority were guaranteed.

Despite everything, his power over the Utes never waned, and while they were under his eye they engaged in no organized warfare. The outbreak in 1879, when Major Thornburg was ambushed and the Agency destroyed, took place while Ouray was absent.

The old chief had received a fair education from the padres at Taos; his Spanish was much more fluent than his English. A rigid Puritan in his personal habits and behavior, he enforced law among the Utes with an iron hand. Kit Carson, Fremont's soft-voiced scout, had been the first United States Agent among the Utes, and Ouray had a vast respect and friendship for him. He appears to have carried his trust in Carson over to other whites much less worthy of it.

Ouray's ready consent to pose should have settled all Jackson's difficulties with the superstitions of the other tribesmen, but smoldering resentment of white treachery showed itself in trivial objections to the camera's "evil eye."

Chief Peah, shown to the *left* in ceremonial dress, was at first very pleased to pose. As may be seen *below,* he wheedled a few friends into a group before a tepee, and Jackson photographed them.

While Peah was busy superintending a distribution of goods to the men at the Agency, Jackson took a picture of his papoose on its carrying-board.

As soon as Peah found out about this, he became very angry and, riding up with some companions, threw a blanket over the camera, protesting, "No sabe picture . . . all die . . . pony die . . . papoose die."

It was clear that Guero, shown *below,* and other conservatives in the tribe had prevailed over Ouray and Peah.

All that afternoon the Utes tried every means short of violence to get hold of the exposed plates and destroy them.

In the evening, a wily, old diplomat known as "Billy" called on Jackson and hinted gracefully that surveyors were not welcome in Ute country. There was no missing the menace behind the soft words, so, very reluctantly, Jackson packed up and headed across country for the Rio Grande.

On the trail up the Rio Grande toward its headwaters and the eastern approach to Baker's Park, Jackson photographed the sharp cut through the mountains at Wagon Wheel Gap (*above*) and a placid reach of the river shown *below*.

A forced march northward to the Lake Fork of the Gunnison brought under the lens Lake San Cristoval (*above*), and a clear view of Uncompahgre Mountain (*below*). Uncompahgre was one of the highest peaks on the northern flank of the San Juan Range.

Jackson's party joined A. D. Wilson's topographers near the little mining settlement of Howardsville at the junction of Cunningham Creek and the upper Rio Las Animas. This town was to be the base for joint explorations among the San Juan peaks. In the picture *above*, Wilson is the bearded man on the right.

There is no record of what the riding mules *below* thought of the mountain trails they would have to negotiate, but the picture gives fine detail of trail equipment.

O white men wintered in San Juan county until 1873. Jim Baker's party of prospectors had been looking for placer gold there in 1861, but the Indians drove them out. Lode prospectors packed equipment up from Santa Fe and began operations in 1870. Arastra Gulch, originally French Gulch and named after Adnah French of the first prospecting party, boasted a single log cabin in 1871, and the first milling in the district was done there at a mule-power mill.

One of the original Baker group, George Howard, returned to Baker's Park in 1871 to found a settlement and build the first house in Howardsville. Shortly before Jackson arrived there, Henry Gill and C. S. Flagler had opened the first mercantile establishment in the county, a combined saloon and general store. Judge Moses Hallett of the Federal Bench had jurisdiction over all western Colorado. He held court at Howardsville in a log house, sixteen feet by twenty, and his docket of cases was not all he had to worry about. The benches in the jury box were so rough and splintery that the jury panel was limited to men who had leather seats in their breeches: "So setting up a qualification," complained the learned justice, "which is without sanction in statute or common law."

Silverton was incorporated as a town in 1874, and so was Parrott City. The population of Silverton grew very rapidly and quite a social life developed there. Colonel Francis Marion Snowden threw open his log house for community dances, and the people of Silverton tripped merrily to the music of J. F. Cotton's violin and his wife's talented hand on the melodeon. Ben Howard thought nothing of packing the mail in winter from Watson's road house at the foot of Grassy Hill all the way up to Silverton, with eighty-odd pounds of meat consigned to the cook at the Highland Mary Mine thrown on his back for good measure.

Near the junction of Rio Las Animas and Cunningham Creek, King Solomon Mountain reared his silver-ribbed bulk, and high up on him was the North Star Mine, with a main lode that averaged forty feet in width. Over beyond Silverton, Sultan Mountain looked out on the panorama of the San Juan, with its buttressing, lateral ranges of the Needles and the Uncompahgre.

Arastra Gulch is shown *above*, and the view *below* was photographed by Jackson in Baker's Park.

Part of the road Ben Howard took on snowshoes with the mail is shown *right*. Cunningham Gulch yawns below the trail.

The miners at the North Star lived in camps near the diggings, like the one pictured *below*.

The view *above* shows the approach to Sultan Mountain. Wilson had decided to make a topographical station on the summit and Jackson accompanied him on the climb.

Silverton (*below*) lay at the foot of a spur running down from Sultan.

The trail up Sultan was steep and soft underfoot. The animals were tied up at timberline, and in usual style the men packed the equipment on their backs for the three thousand feet between the timberline camp and the windy summit. Wilson complained of the cold and worked in his great-coat, as may be seen *right*.

The dark tent is shown *below*, pitched in yet another high place.

Far out to the horizon, the peaks of San Juan stood, row on row.

For the ten days that followed the conquest of Sultan Mountain, Jackson went southward on an adventure which will be described later on. Meanwhile, on his excited return to Baker's Park, Wilson and his men were full of persuasions to make yet another photographic trip. The Wilson party had been wandering about in the region along the San Miguel River, and they all gave such an account of its scenic beauty that Jackson was fairly driven to forget the lateness of the season and have a try at it. So, on September 20, with a hint of snow in the wind, the photographic division packed up and crossed the range from Baker's Park into the San Miguel Valley.

Trout Lake, first known as San Miguel Lake, was photographed against the gorgeously colored peaks that stood between it and Baker's Park.

Of several falls discovered in the canyon below the Lake, the one here pictured was the finest.

The Picture-Maker of the West did not always triumph. The photograph shown *left* was taken, not at the time of the discovery, but a few years afterwards. After a great deal of difficulty in getting his camera down the gorge and into proper position for his first photograph, Jackson found on developing the plate that it had rubbed against the slide of the plate-holder and was completely ruined.

Sleet and snow encouraged speed on the return to Baker's Park. The mules were re-shod, the plates carefully packed and everything was made ready for the homeward trip. At one stage of the road, the wagon which was used to freight the heavier equipment had itself to be disassembled and packed for a while on mule-back, as shown *above*.

Hayden was fond of keeping a photographic record of his Survey personnel. It is presumed that the studies of "Smith, Topographer," and "Lieutenant Jerome," shown respectively left and right, *below*, were made in the Survey camp near Denver.

There should be no trouble identifying the Western character, 1874 model, shown *above*.

THE QUICK AND THE DEAD

THE CITIES OF THE MESA WERE ACCURSED.

For more than twenty summers the rain priests had chanted in vain. The bed of the river was cracked and dry. Across the canyon, by the temple of the Sun Father, the springs had failed. The terraces were barren, and the hot, evil wind had blown away all the soil.

Children had become men, strong men had become toothless and old since first the Rain Bringers had obeyed the angry command of the Divine Ones. The animals had gone far off to the mountains and the hunters returned ever with empty hands. Never again would the Cliff People join in the festival of the green corn.

For centuries they had withstood the attacks of the wild people from the plateaus and plains, but they could not fight against the anger of the gods. Family after family ate the last of its seed corn, bundled up its goods and took the trail away from the Mesa to seek refuge among more fortunate people in whose villages was water.

Under the arch of the cliffs slept the deserted cities. Only the foot of the pack rat stirred in their quiet.

So, more than seven hundred years ago, as white men reckon time, died a great Indian civilization. Its people dispersed themselves among lesser people to mingle their blood with these and sing into alien, ruder myths their dreams of a great past. They survived in bits of pottery left amid the rubble of their cliff-dwellings, in the symbolic rituals of the Pueblos and in the bones that stayed behind in the burial places.

As century followed century the ancient cities became a legend. Wandering Indian hunters stumbled on them and went quickly away for fear of the spirits of the vanished people. When the Spaniard pressed up from Mexico and enforced his authority over the villages of New Mexico and Arizona, he was told stories of golden cities to the north. It was some Spanish explorer who gave a name to the great plateau, fifteen miles long and eight miles across, which rose from the level sands like a "green table." But when the Spaniards toiled across the hot sands, they came upon the poor villages of the Zuni and the Moqui. There was no gold. There were no palaces.

Fray Silvestre Velez de Escalante left his flock at Zuni in the spring of 1776 under orders to find a direct road from Santa Fe to Monterey in California. On August 10, he camped beside a river where there was good pasturage, and he noted in his journal that it was called Las Mancos.

The Mesa Verde and its vicinity became even more remote as the Nineteenth Century opened and progressed. Simpson's discoveries in the Canyon of the Chaco caused no great, learned excitement. The remorseless expansion of the white man from both east and south drove the wild Utes into the maze of dry canyons that criss-crossed Mesa Verde. This desert place was a natural fortress wherein they might still lead the old, free life; and those hardy whites who had entered the valley of the Mancos as early as 1872 were content to leave unexplored the great plateau's labyrinth of washes and ravines.

Early in September, 1874, as Jackson returned to the camp in Baker's Park after completing his work on Sultan Mountain, a full-grown idea was buzzing in his mind. At first, the thing had seemed only another prospector's idle tale, spun from half-understood rumors in the mind of a lonely and imaginative man. But, on the other hand, it might be true.

A week before, he had encountered an old Omaha acquaintance, E. H. Cooper, as that easy-going worthy was driving a burro train of supplies to John Moss's placer camp west of the mouth of the Rio Las Animas. Cooper had been enthusiastic about his boss. He said that Moss knew the country south of the San Juan Mountains like the palm of his hand; that he was a good friend of the Utes and always welcome among them; that he knew of a whole raft of cliff cities deep in the canyons of the Mesa Verde. He had volunteered this last bit after Jackson had told him more or less what the Survey was doing.

Ingersoll was enthusiastic when he heard about Moss. His journalist's nose scented a better story in the basin of the San Juan than could be found among the peaks of the range. And as the men discussed the story around the evening camp-fires, Jackson found himself wanting to believe it. There would be no harm in testing its truth. Wasn't exploration the work of the Hayden Survey?

For better or worse, Jackson and Ingersoll set off down the Rio Las Animas with two of the packers for company and the lightest possible trail equipment. The first two days out were spent in rugged, high country, full of grizzlies and mountain lions, until they reached warmer, pleasanter places in the grassy valleys called Animas Park. Moss's camp was on the Rio La Plata; but as Jackson's group was preparing to turn westward and search for the camp, Moss came riding toward them. Cooper had informed him of the Survey's possible visit, and the courtly prospector had come out to meet and guide them.

John Moss was no fool. He was witty and well-educated, a Western rover by temperament. At present he was superintending prospect operations for a firm of California bankers. Of course he knew all about the cliff cities. They were in Mancos Canyon and he would be happy to guide the gentlemen to them. Nothing easier. Meanwhile, would the visitors come to his camp and give him their heaven-sent votes in a county election which was in progress?

Four votes, solid, for John Moss! Then the polls were closed and they all rode over to Merritt's Ranch for some hospitable entertainment.

John Moss, shown *right,* didn't take much stock in agreements between the United States and the Indians. He made his own private treaties with the Indians, and lived up to their terms.

Merritt's Ranch (*left*) was at this time the only house in the San Juan Basin west of the Rio Las Animas.

The air was crisp and cool and the sky a brilliant blue on the morning after the jollification at Merritt's Ranch. With Moss in the lead, and Cooper tailing along, the Survey party rode down the open valley of the Mancos in holiday mood.

Here and there, beside the trail, were mounds of earth that appeared to be of human shaping and broken shards of pottery in great quantities. All day long, Jackson and Ingersoll eagerly awaited some definite statement from Moss, but none came. It was always "just a bit further." The walls of the canyon began to move in and stretch up; the trail became a rock-strewn nuisance. And it began to draw toward evening.

Moss remained quite confident. Never fear, said he, as they made camp in the canyon, the place is right handy but you'll need a good night's rest before you can climb up to it. One of the packers, Steve, was no longer impressed with the guide's promises and wanted to know precisely where the climb was going to be made. Moss pointed casually toward the very rim of the canyon, a good seven hundred feet above the valley floor.

Steve stared up a while in the waning light.
"Well," he said at last, "I didn't believe a word of it, but there she is."
Everyone rushed to Steve's side and followed his pointing finger. In a shallow cave near the top of the rock wall, they saw the outline of windows and the square bulk of what looked like a two-story house.

Before darkness fell, Jackson and Ingersoll had clambered up the sheer surface by handholds and footholds, and stood in the house of the vanished Cliff Dwellers. There were three rooms on the ground level, separated by partitions of faced sandstone. Traces of a wooden floor were visible between the stories. On the inside, the walls were plastered a dull brick-red color, with a white band along the base, near the floor.

Next morning, after taking many photographs, the excited explorers hurried down the Mancos to the Rio San Juan, photographing as they went. Had they taken time to explore the side canyons near their first discovery, they, and not the Wetherill brothers, would have been the first white men to set foot in Cliff Palace, most magnificent of all the ruins in Mesa Verde.

The site of the camp in Mancos Canyon is shown *above*. From this point, Steve's sharp eyes made out the Two-Story House.

The first photograph ever taken of Mesa Verde cliff-dwellings is reproduced *below*. In this view of the Two-Story House, the standing figure is John Moss.

This picture of Cliff Palace, and the two succeeding views of ruins in the canyon of the Mancos, were made by Jackson at some time subsequent to the snowy December day in 1888 when Richard Wetherill and Charles Mason went hunting stray cattle in the canyon and found a masterpiece of Indian art. All three views show their subjects before restoration.

To the *right* is the central portion of Cliff Palace.

Below is shown the so-called Sandal House.

The view *above,* taken from one of the lesser ruins, gives some idea of the character of the canyon of the Mancos.

As Jackson and his party approached the sandy, alkaline plains near the junction of the Mancos with the San Juan, the broken, weathered walls of the canyon harbored smaller cliff-dwellings, so ruinous that a stiff climb up the perpendicular face shown *right* was necessary to distinguish them from tricks of the wind and sand.

Twenty miles from the mouth of the Mancos, the ruins at Aztec Springs *below* were discovered. They were arranged in what appeared to be a ceremonial relation to what had been once living water. To Moss's amazement, the springs were dry.

The next day's march was westerly toward the dry and barren gulch of the McElmo, a tributary of Hovenweep Creek, which was in turn a tributary of the San Juan. The tower shown *above* was an outwork of the cliff-dwellings to be seen on the left *below*. Ingersoll gave to the small house and its supporting rock, shown on the right *below*, the fanciful name of "Battle Rock."

Along the Hovenweep, ruins were found on the valley floor, as seen *above*.

Although Jackson was sorely tempted to continue his explorations westward, he remembered that he had left unfinished business back in Baker's Park. He said a hasty goodbye to John Moss, after returning to the camp on the Rio La Plata, and promised him that they would continue to search out the secrets of the Cliff Dwellers in 1875. Jackson knew Hayden's mind well enough by now to know that his orders to return to the Rio San Juan would be written before he had finished his tale.

And so it turned out. The season of 1875 found Jackson with a dual commission: first, to carry on from where he had left off along the Hovenweep; second, to visit the Pueblos of the Moqui, south of the San Juan. In their own tongue, these living mesa dwellers were called Hopi, "the peaceful ones," and their seven villages clustered atop or about three mesas in northeastern Arizona.

The camp on the Rio La Plata had been abandoned late in 1874 and the miners had moved to the short-lived town of Parrott City. A picture of Parrott City and its inhabitants is shown *above*. John Moss had received orders from his financial backers to pay them a call in San Francisco and was preparing for the journey as Jackson arrived to claim his services. He recommended Harry Lee in his place as guide and interpreter, and passed the word to his Ute friends that the Jackson party was harmless. In the study *below*, Lee is on the extreme left.

Under Lee's guidance, Jackson proceeded to the McElmo and the Hovenweep, and thence to the San Juan, through a seemingly interminable series of deep, desolate gorges and barren valleys. In the rainy time, these rocky canyons and washes roared with floods, but in summer the greasewood and sagebrush had to send their roots deep down for sustenance. Between the gorges, the tableland stood at an almost uniform height of five hundred feet.

From the mouth of the McElmo, down to the broad wash of the Montezuma, the region yielded no more ruins of any importance. At the arid mouth of the Montezuma, Jackson was surprised to find groves of cottonwoods, brilliantly green, and as he moved westward along the great bluffs which stood over the San Juan at this stage of its course, he was encouraged to further search by a whole series of rock-shelters scattered everywhere along the valley floor and on the walls of the cliffs.

About twelve miles below the mouth of the Montezuma, and occupying almost the entire height of the bluff, a cave ran back in a semi-circular sweep to a depth of more than a hundred feet. Under the great rock dome, which echoed and re-echoed with marvellous distinctness the least word spoken, the Cliff Dwellers had built a little city, shown *below*. On the cement or stucco, spread along the inner walls of one of the houses, Jackson found perfect impressions of the hands of the vanished builders.

Jackson used the 20 x 24 camera shown *left* during this 1875 expedition. In the Seventies of the last century, enlargements were out of the question and Jackson considered his subjects worthy of the largest practicable exhibition.

A short distance above the dry mouth of the Rio de Chelly, the Rio San Juan emerged from a considerable canyon into a pleasant, park-like valley almost a mile in length, only to sink into the even more rugged canyon shown *below*.

Jackson and his companions turned southward and found it hard going over the side canyons of the Rio de Chelly. Presently the valley expanded to a width of almost a mile. The wash of the Chelly skirted one side of this valley, and in the perpendicular bluffs, more than three hundred feet high, where the wash made a wide detour, the Cliff Dweller city shown *above* was perched on a recessed bench some seventy feet above the valley floor.

It was overhung by a solid wall of sandstone.

The whole front of one portion of the town was without any aperture save a few small windows, and the steep slope of the foundation rock made the location a perfect natural fortress.

Over the broad, flat valley that followed, sage-covered, sandy and monotonous, Jackson and his men toiled to the head of the Canyon de Chelly where they found a few Navaho taking advantage of a trickle of water from the mountains eastward to raise corn, pumpkins and melons. From this point the trail branched southwestward and then south, toward the Moqui villages, forty miles away.

Since the great Pueblo revolt in 1680, the Moqui had held aloof, moving their towns higher and higher on the mesas and giving shelter to wanderers who came to them from other, conquered villages. Yet after Jackson and his men made the easy climb to the top of the mesa on which Tewa stood, they were received by the Capitan, or chief, with perfect courtesy. Even the mules received a gracious welcome and were fed to stuffing point with corn.

Nor were the men forgotten. The Capitan led them upstairs in his house and Numpa-yu, "Serpent-that-will-not-bite," served their meal with her own hands.

The photographic tour around the Moqui mesas was like a triumphal progress. In each village, the Capitan received Jackson and his men with a ceremonial meal of baked bread and stewed peaches. Adults and children thronged after Jackson and watched everything he did with eager interest.

The Pueblo of Walpi (*above*) stood on the East Mesa opposite Tewa.

Shupaulovi (*below*) was a comparatively modern Pueblo, supposed to have been founded by colonists from Shongopovi. Both towns are located on the second, or Middle Mesa.

Jackson and his men were fascinated by the gentle manners and perfect poise of their hostess, Num-pa-yu. In Jackson's photograph of her *above,* the dressing of her hair in imitation of the whorls of the squash-blossom indicated that she was marriageable.

The house shown *above* belonged to the Capitan of Shongopovi.

After a moonlight, farewell feast, given by the Capitan of Walpi, the weary Survey party wound up the three-day visit to the Moqui with a sound sleep. Next morning, they began the long journey northward to the Sierra Abajo and Sierra La Sal country in eastern Utah.

Jackson filled a sketch-book with interior views of Moqui houses and thumbnail drawings of characters observed in the villages. The two pages following show reproductions of a selection from these sketches.

Jackson and his men crossed the San Juan and wandered for some days in the region between the Sierra Abajo and the Sierra La Sal. A few, small cliff-houses like the one shown *above* were found in the vicinity of Sierra Abajo. Fortunately for their peace of mind, they were unaware of what had happened to Gardner's Survey party on the Old Spanish Trail near Cold Spring, only a week before.

The 20 x 24 camera is shown *left*, set up for action in Unaweep Canyon.

The rock formation shown *right* was called the "Twins" and stood in the Abajo quadrangle.

After a long, hard push across the heads of the Mesa Verde canyons back to the camp at Parrott City, Jackson discovered that his picture of the red sandstone bluffs shown *below* was much more than a routine photograph. At this very spot, near Sierra La Sal, Gardner's topographers had been pinned against the flinty face of the cliff for two days without water by a band of renegade Indians. The running fire of the renegades had cost the lives of four mules, but the men had managed to escape by night without loss. As Jackson rode into Parrott City, a party was being made up to search for his remains.

Jackson received a bronze medal for his work in constructing the Geological Survey's exhibit at the 1876 Centennial in Philadelphia. He was happy to mold in clay the form and proportions of the cliff cities he had discovered, and it was fitting that the honor should be his, but the task devoured an entire year. And the long days at the Exposition, answering the same foolish questions, over and over again, wearied him into an intense longing for the quiet of the Southwestern desert. Since Hayden and the main parties of the Survey were scheduled to head north in 1877, back to the Wyoming and Montana country that the Indian outbreaks had closed to them previously, Jackson was obliged to make special arrangements for visiting the Southwest on his own.

As he would not have the usual group of packers and assistants, the weight of equipment would have to be cut to a minimum. He ordered, therefore, a supply of highly-touted, experimental dry film, enough for four hundred exposures in his 8 x 10 camera. The stuff was fully guaranteed and was warranted to hold its image for an almost unlimited time before developing. He left Washington for Santa Fe, the film still undelivered; and after a long, overtime wait in Santa Fe he began to despair that it would ever come. But at last it did, and without waiting to give the equipment his usual, careful try-out he took the trail.

He made a stay at Taos; at Fort Defiance where the distribution of annuity goods was being made to the Navaho; at Zuni Pueblo. Under the guidance of Hosta, the San Ysidro Indian who had been Colonel Washington's guide back in 1849, he travelled to the Canyon of the Chaco and explored the ruins in that mirage-haunted valley. There he discovered in a wash at a depth of fourteen feet the famous "Chaco Skull," first human remains ever unearthed of those long-vanished people. He visited the Pueblos of Laguna and Acoma. Wherever he went, his camera recorded the places and the people.

Not a single negative would develop when he returned to headquarters in Washington! The "sensitive, light-weight, negative tissue" had evidently been made to sell and not to work.

In consequence, the Pueblo pictures which follow, with the exception of the altar-piece sketch from Laguna, are reproduced from work done several years afterwards when Jackson's love of the country brought him again to the Southwest.

Above is a view of the Pueblo of Taos, in northern New Mexico, a few miles east of the Rio Grande.

A view of Taos seen from a little distance against its background of mountains is shown *below*.

Beside the clear, cold mountain stream that divides the town, some people of Taos
are seen, grouped under what appears to be a tree-burial.

Children played about an old wagon outside the Pueblo of Laguna, shown *above*.

On his ill-fated 1877 trip, Jackson
sketched the altar-piece (*right*) in the
church at Laguna.

Atop its mesa, ancient Acoma brooded over its glories and its wrongs (*above* and *below*).

ABOARD THE JACKSON SPECIAL

NE fine afternoon, late in the summer of 1879, a new sign was going up on the second floor of a business building at 413 Larimer Street, Denver. It read "William H. Jackson—Photographer."

Around the young proprietor as he stood and stared up at it, swirled the business life of a young and lusty community, a Western city whose population had multiplied by seven in ten years. There was a lift of the spirit in the very air of Denver, "Queen City of the Foothills," set between the high places and the plains. Four daily papers were hawked about her streets; thousands of square miles of rich mining and stock-raising country drew supplies from her shops and warehouses; her four main hotels welcomed better than seventy thousand arrivals a year. Larimer Street housed music stores, vintners who catered to cultivated palates, merchants who dealt in fine carpets and furniture. Yet the city was still filled with men who remembered "Fifty-nine" and had come on one of Ben Holladay's stages to a raw tent-city on a barren plain where, in the words of a contemporary chronicler, "the gambler openly plied his trade, the dance-house and the saloon gathered votaries, the wanton temporizing with decay threw wide the doors of her gilded den." In the rising fortunes of this rich, happy, aspiring city, Jackson hoped to share.

He had returned to Washington late in 1878 from a short, uneventful Survey expedition through Wyoming for what should have been a winter of office routine and domesticity. But Congress in reforming mood had played Providence, consolidated all Government Surveys under one authority, and bade an off-hand farewell to many an efficient public servant. In the new United States Geological Survey, no place had been provided for William Henry Jackson.

Once the first shock was over, he had realized that his joblessness was only another challenge, and he had been accepting challenges since his Vermont boyhood. The West had been good to men with fewer resources than he had, and the answer to his predicament would be found in the West—in Denver. Something more important than the mere accretion of wealth was going on there; and, just as in 1869, he had a hunch that he might succeed in making his artistic ambition and his bread-winning activities serve each other.

The years between 1878 and 1888 were the great decade of railroad promotion and construction, and the peopling of the region between the Missouri River and the Pacific Ocean was largely the work of the railroad builders. The westward running rails brought men and women to the new empire and freighted the produce of their labor back to the mills and factories. In the contemporary view of this phase of westward expansion, the purple sins of the railroads were pretty well condoned and forgotten in the zestful process of empire-building.

For much of this Western railroad activity, the focus was the city of Denver. Colorado had the hard stuff, silver and gold, in addition to its mounting agricultural and stock-raising wealth; and men go where gold is. If the Union Pacific and the older roads took no interest in the Queen City and her future, the men of Colorado would build their own taps to the riches of the Rockies and grow fat thereby.

Jackson returned to the scene as the hastily organized roads were thrusting rails over the mountains to the scene of every new strike, and engaging in a Donnybrook type of competition that brought them all eventually to bankruptcy. But it was fun while it lasted. For twelve years, Jackson followed the construction gangs and rode the new-laid rails, now in a caboose, now in the President's car. It was all one to him so long as he got his pictures. On the railroads he could go to places he had never seen; revisit the mining camps he had climbed to on mule back or on foot; be again in the high places. There was time enough in the long winters to make pictures of local magnates and their families for a living. The days of good weather were his own for the work he could do better than any man of his time, the pictorial chronicle of the West.

The mining towns of Clear Creek and Gilpin Counties were served by the Colorado Central, projected by William Loveland in the hope that he might link the Union Pacific and the Kansas Pacific through his own town of Golden and so make it the metropolis that Denver became. But the gods thought otherwise. Golden remained Golden. And in the late Seventies, the mighty Union Pacific scooped up what was left of the Colorado Central and added it to its great network of rails.

At the forks of Clear Creek, west of Denver, one branch of Loveland's road ran up the northern arm of the Creek to Black Hawk where on a grade of a hundred and thirty-five feet to the mile began the climb around the hills to Central City. On the ascent, the train seemed to hang in space over the roaring chimneys of the smelters below.

Grading in Clear Creek Canyon.

"Inspiration Point" in
Clear Creek Canyon.

[241]

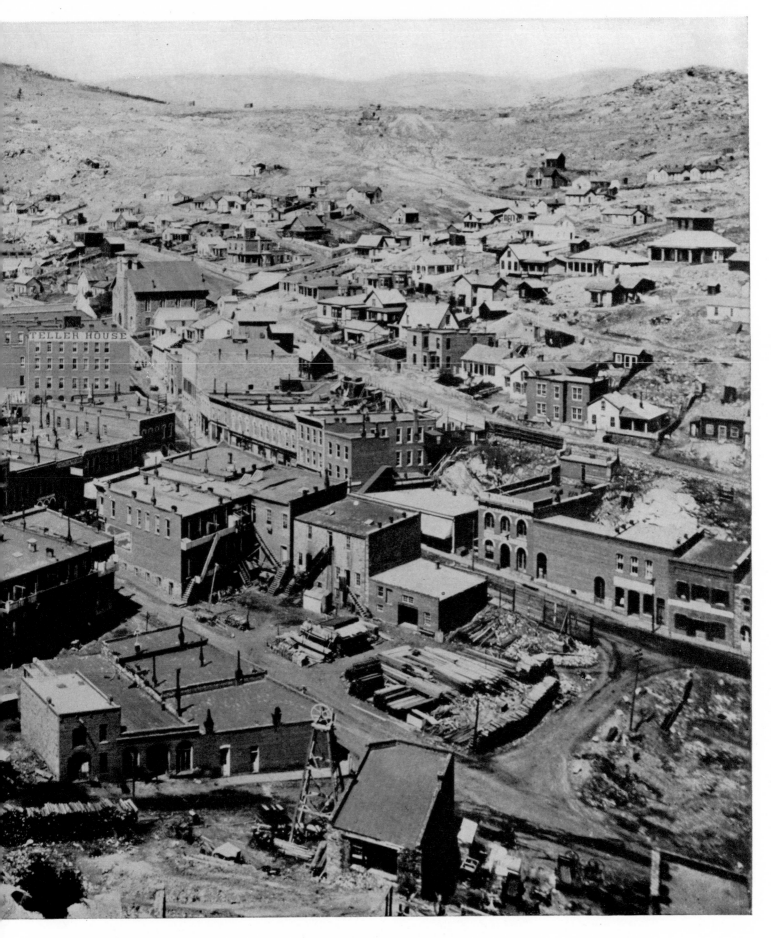

Central City is shown *above*. The Teller House, whose sign appears at about the center of the picture, was the best hotel in the State outside Denver.

Along the southern arm of Clear Creek, the railroad pointed for Idaho Springs where Eastern invalids soothed jangled nerves at the soda springs amid the clatter of the mines above them on the mountain and the din of quartz and concentrating mills on the creek side.

Fourteen miles beyond Idaho Springs was Georgetown, where silver was king. The long "loop" of track into the town was called "the roller coaster that got you somewhere." To Jackson, who remembered his troubles with mules, toll-gates and snow-slides at Georgetown, back in '73, the thriving community with its five churches, two banks, its school and its opera house was like the work of genii.

Rails southward from Denver
eased the road to Pike's Peak for
local people and an increasing
throng of summer tourists from
the East. The "Seal and Bear"
were in the Garden of the Gods.

Viewed from a point near Colorado City, Pike's Peak defied the tenderfoot to attempt a climb to the summit.

But the picture shown *above*, taken on the trail near Windy Point, proves that the ascent was not too hard. If the lady in the plumed hat could make it, others could.

The final step in the taming of the Peak is shown *above*. In its day, the Manitou and Pike's Peak Cog Railway was the most remarkable railroad in the world. It lofted the tourist above the clouds with a minimum of effort.

South and west of Denver, the story of the railroad was the story of another strong-willed builder who did well before the speculators picked his bones.

William Palmer, for all his Quaker conscience, raised and commanded the Fifteenth Pennsylvania Cavalry, and served from 1861 until Jefferson Davis was captured. After conspicuous service at Antietam, Chickamauga and on the march to Atlanta, he could not return to his old life as private secretary to an Eastern magnate. Full of the gust of the times, he projected a trunk line running north and south that would link Denver with Mexico City and levy on the wealth of the whole Southwest. His road, the Denver and Rio Grande, had reached Pueblo by 1872, but in the days after the Panic of 1873 all construction was halted. Palmer waited restlessly for new capital. His dream could come true only if he were able to push his rails through Raton Pass, due south of Pueblo, and the only practicable path southward across the mountains. But a new prospect opened when a great strike was made at Leadville in 1877. The possibility of rich freights from that district made feasible an extension of the Denver and Rio Grande westward through Leadville to Ogden, Utah, and the eventual Pacific. And here was another dilemma. Leadville could be reached only through the Royal Gorge, that narrow cleft in the mountains of southern Colorado through which the upper Arkansas tumbled at the start of its course to the Mississippi.

There was room in the Gorge for only a single line of track. When Palmer's construction crews arrived at last in the Royal Gorge (*above*), they found the pass occupied by graders and gunmen of a rival road.

For three years the issue was joined in the field with picks and bullets, and in the courts with suits, pleas and injunctions.

Early in 1880, the directors of Palmer's own road signed away his dream of an international trunk line to Mexico when they surrendered their rights to Raton Pass in exchange for a free hand in the Royal Gorge and the mountains of Colorado.

At Salida, fifty-four miles by rail beyond the Royal Gorge, the main line of the Denver and Rio Grande headed for Grand Junction by way of Leadville. The view *right* shows South Park from the vicinity of the Kenosha Hills, just beyond Salida.

A branch turned off at the entrance to Brown's Canyon and climbed on a grade of four hundred and six feet to the mile toward the iron mines at Calumet. A work train is shown *below,* halted beneath the Castle Rock near Calumet.

Beyond Leadville, where the famous Horace Tabor held forth as first citizen and Mayor, the railroad crossed Crane's Park (*above*) at the western end of Tennessee Pass. The round objects on the right are kilns for burning charcoal.

Westward of Tennessee Pass, between Leadville, pouring out fantastic wealth from the Little Pittsburgh and the Matchless mines, and Aspen, equally rich in silver and lead, the tracks of the Colorado Midland were protected by snow sheds where the drifts were expected to be deepest. In the view of Hagerman Pass, shown *below*, the train is just emerging from one of these sheds.

In Hagerman Pass, Jackson saw the snow plow at work.

When passengers on the main line of the Denver and Rio Grande reached Eagle River Canyon (north of Leadville and very near the Mountain of the Holy Cross), they gawked up at the shaft houses and homes of the miners that perched on the heads of the tunnels. The steel-rope carry, seen at the *right* in this view of the Ben Butler Mine, saved a long walk down to the railway level.

The Eagle Bird Mine was a near neighbor of the Ben Butler.

Gloomier than the canyon of the Arkansas was the canyon of the Grand River, now called the upper Colorado. The "Portals" in Grand River Canyon are shown *above*.

Echo Cliffs *above* were in the canyon of the Grand River. The engineers were fond of entertaining passengers with the blast of the locomotive whistle under the loom of the cliffs.

Beyond Grand Junction, where the Grand and Gunnison Rivers joined, the train pushed across two hundred and fifty miles of desert and climbed the Wasatch Range into the fertile valley of Price River, Utah. Through the Castle Gate in Price River Canyon (*below*) Albert Sydney Johnston marched his soldiers on their homeward journey after the punitive expedition against the Mormons in 1857 and 1858.

A branch line to the Alta Mines cut across Little Cottonwood Canyon from Bingham, some eight miles south of Salt Lake City. The view *above* shows the head of Little Cottonwood. The main line continued on through the Mormon capital to Ogden, where the rails turned toward the Pacific.

The railroads went wherever there was wealth to be tapped or fertile land to be opened up for settlement. In west-central Colorado, there was gold and silver and coal, so narrow-gauge tracks were laid from Salida junction up, up in dizzy spirals until they paused breathlessly at the eleven-thousand-foot elevation of Marshall Pass before making an equally exciting descent to the Gunnison River. In the picture *above*, taken high in Marshall Pass in 1882, the author of the present volume is shown, seated on the rear platform of the coach. Above him, standing, is his mother.

The men seen *above* were fishing for trout in the Gunnison, just outside the prosperous town of Sapinero, where a branch line cut off to Lake City.

Sapinero stood at the head of the Black Canyon of the Gunnison, where the waters of the river took on a deep, sea-green hue and the dark walls were only occasionally relieved by the red of sandstone and the green of cedar and piñon. One of these touches of color was Currecanti Needle (*right*), a brilliant red from base to point, in whose shadow the Indians of the vicinity once held their councils.

The narrow-gauge line from Salida to Grand Junction might boast the wealth of Lake City and the beauty of the Gunnison Valley, but the road from Alamosa to Silverton was rich with the freight of the great new mines of the San Juan and in the beauty of the southwestern peaks, canyons and valleys.

It had been less than ten years since Jackson had come south to this country as explorer and discoverer, yet the character of the San Juan country had already changed.

Ten miles from Wagon Wheel Gap (see page 198) one of the most hopeful mining towns in Colorado had opened up, and there was great excitement over the high percentage of gold to silver in the yield of its ore. This was Creede, and the contrasts in its architecture are well illustrated in the view of Main Street shown *below*.

The other end of Main Street, Creede, is pictured *above*. The sign on the wall to the left, with an heirloom look to it as if it had seen service before in more effete surroundings, bears the legend "Lager Beer."

A great bend of the railroad around the side of a mountain above the Los Pinos Valley was known as "Phantom Curve" (*below*).

After stops at Chama and Durango, the railroad headed up the valley of the Rio Las Animas. This was no longer the lonely place that Jackson and Ingersoll had found on their trip to the country of the Cliff Dwellers. It was almost bustling with new settle-

ments and homesteading. The rails clung to the cliffs midway of their height in Animas Canyon (*above*).

The work train shown *above* was one of the many "Jackson Specials", with which the photographer was furnished by the railroad companies. The picture was taken in Animas Canyon.

Long before the railroad came to Silverton, enterprising individuals had thrown a web of toll-roads over this part of the San Juan country, and had grown fat from the profits. Over the Ouray-Silverton toll-road, shown *above*, and similar roads, burros packed ore down to Silverton at twenty-five dollars a ton.

LATE in the Eighteen-eighties, the rails gave Jackson his chance to see still another West—the golden country of California. From Ogden the swaying cars hurried across the great desert which, forty years before, had wasted the strength and youth of men and women who went overland by wagon train. Each mile of sand and sagebrush had known tragedy; each landmark and way station along the line was a living memory of the California Trail. Humboldt Valley—Gravelly Ford—Mirage—Reno (now flourishing as the junction point for a whole hatful of railroads to the Nevada mines)—Truckee, where the great mass of the Sierra Nevada closed in the horizon! And then the road began the big climb, up past the lakes—Tahoe—Donner, with its memory of starvation and cannibalism—under snow sheds where the panting of the two engines roared and reverberated—up to Summit, the station on the divide where little rivers rose to come at last to the great stream of the Sacramento.

In a different manner and by a different route, he was entering the state he had come to as a bullwhacker, so many years before. Sacramento, Benicia, the Straits of Carquinez, Oakland Pier, the wharves of San Francisco! Then southward to the San Joaquin Valley, with a journey from Berendo to the scenic grandeur of the Yosemite Valley; southward again through the well-remembered Mohave Desert to the places where a long line of missions testified even in decay to the genius and vision of Junipero Serra.

Square-riggers were moored at the San Francisco piers.

But Jackson had no great and abiding interest in cities. The Yosemite Valley was a little more than two hundred and fifty miles away, by rail and by stage, and there he would go. Thirty-odd years before, the Indians had been driven from it; their memory remained only in the legends and stories which clung to every rock, canyon and stream in the incomparable valley.

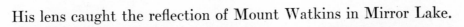

From the floor of the valley he photographed the summit of Half Dome in its sheer rise of almost forty-nine hundred feet.

His lens caught the reflection of Mount Watkins in Mirror Lake.

Bridal Veil Falls, dropping six hundred and twenty feet from majestic, granite walls, gave Jackson the subject for one of his most striking photographs.

Almost as if they had been hewn by human hands, the Three Brothers (*above*) slanted up to a height of thirty-nine hundred feet. The whole valley, with its towering heights and the boom and mist of waterfalls, seemed unreal and haunted.

In the Mariposa Grove and southward, Jackson for the first time saw and photographed these giant trees.

From crest to river, the Great Falls of the Yosemite descend for half a mile. The Upper Fall is the height of nine Niagaras. Jackson's eye for composition of scenes brought this splendid picture into being.

After leaving Yosemite, he could not see the Joshua Yuccas near Cajon Pass without a rueful memory of old Sam McGannigan and the horse drive, and how hot and thirsty he had been on the way across the Mohave, bound for Omaha and the start of his career.

Around the Spanish Missions in California, from San Francisco de Asis to San Diego, the Indians had set up villages in which they lived and learned from the friars the arts of peace. But under Mexican rule, the happy system decayed, and by the time Jackson saw the Missions they were only the shells of what they had been. The gardens were untended and the plaster was flaking from the walls.

Father Serra had founded San Juan Capistrano (*above*) in 1776. The Mission of San Luis Rey (*below*) was founded in 1798.

TRAILS OF MEMORY

ACKSON stood at the window of his Denver office and looked out; first at the crowded, busy street, and then over the roofs of the city to the mountains.

A quarter of a century had passed since, urging the bull train over the rough trail, he had first seen the high places. Then he had had only a dingy notebook and a pencil with which to record what he saw; but now, in the last decade of the Nineteenth Century, he stood recognized as the outstanding photographer of a West which was already a part of history. The desk behind him was piled high with orders from all parts of the world for prints of his famous views. Every owner of a stereoscope knew his name. Railroads glorified their routes with published collections of Jackson photographs.

It had been a long and happy trail that had taken him from the jumping-off place on the Missouri River back in 1866, to this comfortable office of the W. H. Jackson Photograph and Publishing Company. He recalled the sketch he had made of an immigrant family on the train, seeking like himself and Rock Rounds and Billy Crowl the better life beyond the frontier.

The memories came crowding. How lonesome he had been in Echo Canyon, and how
glad to jaw with the railroad men who gave him lifts on that first trip to the Utah Canyons in '69!

The way the roof of the Mormon Tabernacle stood up in the valley, like the bottom of an overturned boat! That was before they had built the Temple. He remembered watching the quarrymen at work on the Temple's stones in Cottonwood Canyon.

The Survey days had been happy days. The brilliant, irascible Hayden had kept them all on their toes. They had camped at Three Springs, Idaho, on the road back from Yellowstone, and the old man had been positively genial.

But wherever they camped, meal-time was always a merry occasion.

In Jackson's memory, Yellowstone was the greatest adventure. To see for the first time the Jupiter Terrace at the Mammoth Hot Springs . . .

. . . and the roaring Yellowstone River just above the Upper Falls! The fifteen-second exposure had smoothed the rapids in the foreground down to a quiet surface, like a lake's.

Heart Lake, its shore a powder of volcanic ash, lay to the southwest of Yellowstone Lake on the way to the geysers.

And once in the geyser basins, the Lone Star had been worth the trouble it had taken to find it.

When last he had seen Old Faithful, in 1883, the geyser had been as "accommodating" as Hayden had long ago described it.

Ouray was dead. He had died in 1880, but his wife Chipeta, "the charitable one," was still living on the Ute reservation. Jackson treasured the pipe of peace with which the old chief had honored him; it hung on his office wall.

Washakie was far from dead. He was still as dominant over his Shoshones as he had been when Jackson photographed him among his head men in 1870.

Chief Joseph of the Nez Percés, "Thunder-Coming-From-The-Water-Up-Over-The-Land," had had a Roman dignity, even in defeat. Greatest and noblest of Indian warriors, he had fought a magnificent Fabian campaign in 1877, surrendering only in the face of odds of twenty to one.

In that same year, 1877, the soldiers had gathered up a group of the Bannacks and held them under guard at Camp Brown, Wyoming, lest the news of Joseph's early successes strike an answering fire in them.

He remembered the road under Hanging Rock in Clear Creek Canyon, for that road had led to the high places and the first photographing of the Mountain of the Holy Cross. Nor could he forget the little "Jackson Special" that had taken him wherever the rails ran.

Sometimes he had ridden in the comparative grandeur of a coach through Alpine Pass (*right*), or around the Phantom Curve (*below*) on the road to Silverton. More often, though, he had thought it fortunate if the "Jackson Special" boasted a caboose with a red-hot stove.

It could get good and cold in the Colorado passes. Lizard Head Pass was eleven thousand feet high at the summit, where the railroad began its zig-zag descent to the San Miguel Valley.

Remembered faces! The bland face of an anonymous mule, peering out through a lumber pack consigned to the mines! The bearded face and dignified hat of an old prospector he had met at Parrott City, back in 1875! He wondered if the old man had ever made his strike.

When last he had been in the Southwest, "Navaho Jake" had been making a few dollars guiding tourists to the Moqui villages, but those proud, secretive people still held to their ancient ways. He had heard that Num-pa-yu was now esteemed the greatest pottery maker among the Moqui.

Near the Pueblo San Juan, at Chamita, there was an old mill that barely creaked around in the languid flow of the stream.

The people of Pueblo San Juan were Christians, a kind, generous people whose character had won for their town the title of "San Juan de Los Caballeros." They worshipped in the Mission church shown *above*. But their brothers at Walpi still celebrated the ancient rites. Jackson recalled vividly the dance of the Antelope priesthood he had photographed there.

The Pueblo of Laguna had been a place for dreaming under the burning sun; Montezuma Canyon with its relics of the older, vanished people had been an arid valley of ghosts.

From Montana creeks, where flumes carried gold-bearing gravel down from the mines . . .

. . . through the sullen gloom of the waste country about Great Shoshone Falls . . .

. . . to Eagle Crag on the Virgin River in Utah . . .

. . . and the Grand Canyon of the Colorado near the big bend above Peach Springs, Arizona, life had been a challenge to his strength and spirit and skill.

JACKSON turned from the window and walked to his desk. In his pictures the pioneer age would have an immortality. The mining captains and the railroad kings would have their golden day and depart, but his work would live. He was sure of it. Where else could future generations see the wild majesty of the Western land; the grim faces of its aboriginals, free and proud in their own country; the thrust outward of restless white men by road and rail from the Mississippi to the Pacific?

High and far, from canyon rim and mountain top, his camera had looked out on the West.

YELLOWSTONE REGION

Inset map labels:
Gallatin
Yellowstone
Jupiter Terrace
Mammoth Hot Springs
Gardiner
Tower Falls
Tower Creek
Madison
Gibbon
Cascade Creek
GRAND CANYON
Mt. Washburn
Lower Falls
Upper Falls
Fountain
Middle Geyser Basin
Lower Geyser Basin
CONTINENTAL
Grotto
Giant
Castle
Grand
Giantess
Old Faithful
Firehole
Beehive
Upper Geyser Basin
Yellowstone Lake
Shoshone Lake
DIVIDE
Shoshone Grand Basin
Heart Lake
Miles
5 10 15 20

Main map labels:
Fort Benton
Missouri
Helena
Virginia City
Ft. Ellis
(MONT)
Yellowstone
Mt. Blackmore
Gardiner
Henry's Lake
Yellowstone Lake
Grand Teton
Little Gros Ventre
Jackson's Lake
(IDAHO)
Henry's
Teton
Snake
Port Neuf
Fremont Peak
Ft. Hall
WIND RIVER
Promontory Point
Corinne
Ogden
Bear
to Montana
Horse
Green
South Pass
Little Sandy
Big Sandy
Ft. Bridger
UNION
Great Salt Lake
WASATCH
Echo Canyon
Blacks
Henry
Salt Lake City
Weber
UINTA
(UTAH)
Tampa
Utah Lake
Green
Nephi
TRAIL
Sevier
to Santa Fe
Colorado
(COL)
Gunnison
UNCOMPAHGRE
Mt. Sultan
San Miguel
Silverton
BAKER'S PARK
SALT LAKE & LOS ANGELES
Las Vegas
Virgin
ELK
MONTEZUMA
LA SAL
ABAJO
Rio
Dolores
Animas
Mesa Verde
Hovenweep
Mancos
San Juan
Colorado
NEVADA
CALIFORNIA
Sacramento
Placerville
Sacramento
San Francisco
San Francisco de Asis
SIERRA NEVADA
Yosemite Valley
San Joaquin
Monterey
MOHAVE DESERT
OLD SPANISH TRAIL
Cajon Pass
Los Angeles
Santa Ana
San Juan Capistrano
San Luis Rey
San Diego
Hopi MESAS
Rio de Chelly
Chaco Canyon
Zuni
Laguna
MESAS
Acoma
(ARIZONA)
(NEW
Gila

Le Roy H. Appleton